The Secrets to Living a Fantastic Life

Two Survivors Reveal the 13 Golden Pearls They've Discovered

FOREWORD BY
Jack Canfield
Author of the #1 New York Times Bestseller
Chicken Soup for The Soul

WRITTEN BY

Dr. Allen Lycka and Harriet Tinka

Printed in the United States of America

First Printing, 2020

ISBN: 978-1-989849-00-2

Library of Congress Control Number: 2020908712

CJSM Publishing

1425 – 10665 Jasper Avenue

Edmonton, Alberta, Canada T5J 3S9

www.DrAllenLycka.com

The Secrets to Living a Fantastic Life

Two Survivors Reveal the 13 Golden Pearls They've Discovered

"It's not what happens…
It's what you do with what happens."
- Epictetus, about 2,000 years ago.

Two lives changed, irreversibly, in an instant, by devastating events…but rather than be destroyed, these two individuals faced the ensuing challenges, embracing them as turning points. Seizing the second chances before them with both hands, they chose the path to "Living a Fantastic Life." In doing so, they discovered "13 Golden Pearls" to guide them…which they are eager to now share with you - to inspire you for your own journey.

DEDICATION

Although all books have many contributors,
this book would not be without
Dr. David Martz
Haines Ely
Amber

CONTENTS

FOREWORD
by Jack Canfield

I interviewed two wonderful people - Dr. Allen Lycka and Harriet Tinka - on "Talking About Success." Dr. Allen Lycka is a world-class cosmetic dermatologist whose life collapsed in 2003 when he suddenly developed a foot drop.

Following extensive testing and enduring further deterioration of his condition, he was diagnosed with Lou Gehrig's disease (ALS), which is a terminal diagnosis. He didn't like hearing that – so he questioned it. That's right; he pulled himself together and questioned the diagnosis.

Harriet, his co-author, is a former Vogue model and youth counselor who experienced a different type of trauma. She endured being kidnapped, stabbed, and left for dead.

Neither were destroyed by these experiences. Just like metal is tempered by extreme elements, so were they. And that's led to a whole new philosophy of life and a book that these guys are now doing together, called The Secrets of Living a Fantastic Life... Discover the 13 Golden Pearls.

And they are experts on what they do. It's become their mission to share these metaphorical golden pearls to realize what it takes to live a fantastic life with their book, public speaking, videos, and coaching so that others may benefit.

Both authors have risen above two very difficult and challenging experiences in their respective lives.

Here are just three of the '13 golden pearls' they share:

empowerment, thankfulness, and forgiveness - three pearls that can enhance any life:

1. Empowerment, which means feeling good, feeling good about yourself, just living the life and letting it go.

2. Thankfulness is about being grateful for everything you have. By being grateful for everything, you change from being self-centered into being a person who is more giving, and you can experience that much more. This changes the world, which changes the focus from you to something better.

3. Forgiveness – the act of forgiving helps the forgiver as much as the one that is forgiven. Holding hate and pain inside yourself is like drinking poison and trying to hurt the other person. Forgiveness is not for the person you're giving it to but is a gift to yourself. It frees your soul and makes you that much healthier and better.

Dr. Lycka and Harriet teach that a person can forget everything and run or face everything and rise-up. I like that. That's beautiful, very good. That's a lot of wisdom but encapsulated in humor.

Dr. Lycka and Harriet are on a mission because of cataclysmic life changes. I've done a lot of studying of people that have had what are called "near-death experiences," where they've been pronounced clinically dead. And then they come back and say, "I went through a tunnel. I saw a being of light, and I had to review my life and look at all the places where I wasn't loving and kind, and maybe I got some wisdom from these advanced beings in another dimension."

These guys didn't have that experience exactly, but they were nearly dead, and Dr. Lycka was diagnosed as going to be dead. They went through their own "tunnels." It sounds like they've come back with a similar shared mindset as a result. They all come back, wanting to be of service. They all come back with a greater sense of love.

Those who come back from a near-death experience come back wanting to contribute and have less fear of death. It sounds like these guys have achieved kind of the same thing. It is now their life mission to share and help.

I love what these guys are doing, the book is great, and the work they're doing is important.

— *Jack Canfield*, author of the #1 New York Times Bestseller *Chicken Soup for The Soul.*

INTRODUCTION

I am going to make a bold prediction. You bought this book because something is a challenge in your life. Perhaps you have relationship issues. Maybe you're ill. Maybe things in life have not worked out the way you thought they would. Life can be tremendously cruel. Or maybe you are on a quest to a higher path. But let me ask you some simple questions:

Are you a victim? Have you been overtaken by a victim mentality? Bruce Lipton said, "Victim consciousness robs us of our creative ability." Wouldn't you sooner be a victor and conquer all your problems?

The solution is surprisingly simple. It's to adopt a new mindset: "It's not what happens to you; it's what you do with what happens." Taking on this mindset may be challenging at first, but once you do, life will be enormously different. Everything will change – for the better. Epictetus, an ancient Greek, realized this about 2,000 years ago.

Both Harriet Tinka, my co-author, and I have lived through immense adversity. And by doing so, we came out better and stronger than we were before. We learned and lived the philosophy taught by Epictetus.

What kind of adversity did we suffer?

Harriet Tinka is an accountant, empowerment youth worker, marathon runner, and a former fashion model who was kidnapped and savagely attacked by a male classmate while a student at the University of Calgary. The attacker left her for dead. During her convalescence, she initially felt embittered. But she chose hope, not hate, and learned *The Secrets to Living a Fantastic Life.*

My story is equally unnerving. I have developed a reputation as a world-class cosmetic dermatologist, thought leader, and philanthropist in my 40 years practicing medicine. My life imploded in 2003 when I suddenly developed a right foot drop while on vacation, ironically, at the 'happiest place on earth.' Upon extensive testing, I was diagnosed with ALS (Lou Gehrig's disease) and told I would be dead in six months.

Initially crushed by this diagnosis, I pulled myself together and questioned the opinion. Through my persistence, I overcame the devastation, found my correct diagnosis, and discovered *The Secrets To Living a Fantastic Life.* I learned to thrive.

We both came to this same realization, independently.

Because adversity poisons some and strengthens others, we would like to accompany you on your journey. Heat tempers steel, making it stronger. Harriet and I have both been tempered, learned how to take hold of our second chances and would like to share our experiences.

We share this all in the dialogue we had as we wrote this book – the conversation of two close friends. And we've become so close that we finish each other's sentences. Scary, right?

And within as little as 30 days, if you genuinely apply these principles, your life will be transformed. Guaranteed. Because even if you try just one thing, your life experience will be enhanced immeasurably.

The Importance of the Stories in this Book

Harriet and I were faced with a dilemma when writing this book – how can we even begin to share the important pearls we learned through our lives and the events we experienced? Well, after thinking long and hard – and weighing the consequences –

we decided to have a feature story to highlight the key points of each chapter.

These stories are to get you to think, laugh, cry, and be a part of the process. It is important to note that these stories are not just about Harriet and me. They speak on all elements of the human experience.

And, to a large extent, they are meant to be about you. So, in future books, we welcome your stories.

You can send them to www.LivingAFantasticLife.com. We promise to look at each and every one.

- Dr. Allen Lycka

A Special Note: It is said that when the student is ready, the teacher will arrive. The teacher that arrived for Harriet and me was Rusti L Lehay who made our words and thoughts dance. If you would like her help to do the same for you, contact her at rusti@rustilehay.ca. Call or text 780.278.7120.

Thank you also to Kelly Falardeau - Mixx & Koki Productions - Amazon Best-Seller Strategist admin@KellyFalardeau.com

Authors' Stories

Dr. Lycka and Harriet Tinka have incredible stories to share.

Dr. Lycka has, for over 30 years, excelled in the medical industry and is known as a world-renowned leader in the fields of cosmetic surgery, dermatology and skin health.

He has done over 10,000 liposuction surgeries and over 100,000 skin cancer surgeries, saving the lives of thousands of skin cancer patients and those with skin problems. He won the prestigious Consumer Choice Award for 16 consecutive years and was named Philanthropist of the year in 2013.

As co-author, it is Dr. Lycka's goal to help you live a fantastic life too.

Dr. Lycka's Story

It was a beautiful spring day in 2003. My wife, Lucie, and I had taken a short vacation with our youngest daughter and her friend to enjoy Disneyland, and while walking in the Magic Kingdom, Lucie turned to me and asked, "What's wrong with you, hon?"

I checked my mental checklist. For once, I hadn't said, done, or even thought anything wrong. I realized I didn't have the faintest idea what she was talking about.

I was confused. "What do you mean?"

She said, "Your foot is flapping."

Now that really befuddled me. Not only did I not know what Lucie meant, but now I didn't think we were talking the same language. My wife's primary language is French, mine – English. So, I must admit, episodes of miscommunication like this had occurred many times in the past.

"What do you mean?" I asked again.

"Listen to your foot."

By the perplexed look on my face, she knew that she had to explain. "Don't you hear it? Your foot is flapping against the pavement with every step you take. You don't lift it when you're walking. You have a dropped right foot. It should lift automatically. You need to get it checked out."

I resisted. "I'm tired and it's hot." It was a hot and humid 33 degrees centigrade (around 100 degrees F).

"No, that doesn't explain it. Did you have a stroke?"

Well, no stroke I know of would be like this, so I retorted back, "Dear, you're a doctor. You know strokes don't show up like this."

"Well, something is wrong," she insisted. "When you get back, you better get it checked out." She wasn't kidding.

So began the crisis. I sought out dozens of specialists who were equally perplexed. So, I commenced the million-dollar work-up – CAT scans, MRIs, brain scans, a lumbar puncture, an EMG, a bone marrow aspiration, pulmonary function tests, a gazillion blood tests, and so on. The first thought I had was a slipped disc in my neck, but when tests showed nothing, they assumed I had a "space-occupying lesion," which in lay terms means a brain cancer. But further testing showed nothing was wrong. Absolutely nothing. They were perplexed.

Then came the bombshell. One neurologist had me come to his office and said, "You better be sitting down when I tell you this."

"Why, what's wrong?" timidly whispering, I slumped in the chair, now thoroughly frightened.

"You have Amyotrophic Lateral Sclerosis, ALS (Lou Gehrig's disease)," he said, matter of factly, "and you have six months to live."

"Get your affairs in order," he said.

I was confused and dazed. How could a flapping foot be a death sentence? It made absolutely no sense.

"Is there a way to confirm the diagnosis?"

"Yes," he said, "Autopsy."

I can't express in words the revulsion I felt toward this man at that moment. Yes, I was angry. I could have chewed the heads off of nails at that moment. I felt like leaping up and strangling him. How could an educated man be so callous, so cruel?

I had a dropped foot. To prove him wrong, I was not going to die.

In a daze, I stumbled out of his office and went home. I then began to react emotionally and physically to this diagnosis. I didn't know it at the time, but I began to experience the phases of dying that were identified by Elizabeth Kübler-Ross in *Of Death and Dying*.

First, I reacted with anger. How could this be? I was only 52 years old. I was at the peak of my career, my life. I was too young. It was so unfair.

I plunged harder into my work. I was in Kübler-Ross's second phase – denial. I worked like a demon. If I was going to die, I'd have something to show for it at the end.

I then became depressed. I couldn't sleep. I couldn't eat. My work began to suffer. For the first time, I thought of suicide.

I bargained with God. *I will do anything if you take this away.*

I became angry. I was in full denial.

It is true that when your life is near the end, you begin to see things more clearly. You begin to see patterns, things you could never see otherwise. You reach out. So, I began a new journey – a journey to find my true diagnosis. I wasn't going down without a fight. I did not accept the death sentence of ALS.

Doctor Google did not exist in 2003. Going to the internet then was laborious. I searched thousands of sites. Somehow, after months with the Grim Reaper breathing down my neck, I stumbled upon the story of Dr. David Martz, a hematologist in Colorado Springs, Colorado. David had a story similar to mine, but he had deteriorated much more rapidly to being bedridden within months. He was on his deathbed when Dr. William Harvey, a chronic disease specialist, heard of David's plight and came to see him. Dr. Harvey finally made the correct diagnosis. He started him on antibiotics, and, like Lazarus, David arose from the dead.

I was convinced that both David and I had chronic Lyme disease, not ALS. Dr. Martz started a clinic in Colorado called the Rocky Mountain Chronic Disease clinic to help others. When I read about this, I knew I had to see him.

I called him on a Saturday, getting a hold of him through the local Methodist hospital. We chatted. After a while, he asked, "Why don't you come down to see me?"

"When?" I asked.

"Why not Monday?" he replied.

"That's our Thanksgiving," I protested. Thirty people were coming for Thanksgiving dinner.

"Doesn't Canada have any planes?" he retorted.

I turned to my wife, Lucie, "Dear, I am going to miss Thanksgiving."

"Where are you going this time?" she asks.

"No, dear, I am not going to another meeting. I'm going to Colorado Springs."

"Why?"

"I think I found the answer."

She turned a 180. "Of course you must go. I can handle 30 people. Remember, I came from a French family. For me this is nothing. You must go."

I booked my flight out on Monday for an appointment to see David the next day. I gave him my flight details. I flew into Denver without incident, then got on a little commuter plane late in the day. What a mistake. Late in the day in Colorado, the winds get up to hurricane gusts. It happens all the time. Hot, moist air rises from the desert, and when it does, especially by the mountains, it cools. Turbulence and storms result.

On the way there, I got caught in one of these horrific storms. Although it was only 25 minutes long, the flight seemed like an eternity. The plane bobbed up and down like a cork caught in a tidal wave.

It was like being on a Drop of Doom carnival ride with a never-ending ticket. With each gigantic up, there was an equally gigantic down. And this meant my stomach immediately went up to my mouth and expelled its contents over and over.

That plane ride became a metaphor for the journey I had been on, and in the end, I all but crawled off the plane.

And as I got to the end of the gangway, a familiar voice greeted me. "Hi, Allen."

It was David. Relief flooded through me as the energy and kindness of this man enveloped me immediately in a hug that assured me all my problems would soon be solved. He led me to his car sitting there on the tarmac. We went to a coffee shop, chatting all the way, and talked on into the evening. People seeing us would have sworn we knew each other for years. He dropped me off at the hotel after 2:00 AM. In parting, "I think history is repeating itself," he said.

The next day, I saw him at his office bright and early.

Ordering a blood test, he confirmed my diagnosis of Chronic Lyme disease and started me on treatment, which stabilized my disease and is the reason I'm alive 16 years after my supposed demise.

I would occasionally run into that neurologist in the elevator of our shared office building after the original diagnosis. I'd quip, "Here I am, it's a year (or two or three) and I'm not dead yet. Brilliant deduction."

Since, my medical history has been up and down. Another physician, Dr. Haines Ely, has often been helpful with thoughts and suggestions. In fact, many were radical, but they preserved my old body and helped me through many, many storms. Haines, sadly, recently passed away.

As for me - I've been living on borrowed time. Just think – I had been diagnosed with ALS – Lou Gehrig's disease – a guaranteed death sentence - and now I had a chance to live my life, a more fantastic life.

To this day, I vividly remember my journey to find the dedication and compassion of David and the moment of being treated properly – because it was the moment I emerged from the mental fog that had almost destroyed my life. It was accompanied by a feeling of euphoria, of internal bliss, of internal awakening.

That's when I realized that I had received a "golden ticket," a second chance to live more abundantly. And although I had been afflicted, I actually had been blessed. I finally knew God's plan for me. And that I could help others find solutions for their problems without the hardship or difficulty I had encountered. Or at the very least minimize the time spent in suffering.

Let's turn now to Harriet for her story.

Harriet Tinka

I was hobbling slowly on crutches in the hospital hall.

I made my way towards the waiting room, wrapped up in what the hospital staff called the "Johnny gown." This gown left me partially exposed to strangers and scared me to the bone in its undermining any dignity I wished to possess.

I have no idea why they invented such a contraption. I had no control over my life anymore: a prisoner wearing a wristband with a serial number.

As I sat down, I could hear the voices of patients in agony in the examining room. It was strangely comforting to know that others were also fighting their own demons.

A squeaky noise from a distance diverted my attention. A joyful little girl appeared propelling herself in a wheelchair. I wanted to be alone. I made no eye contact, hoping she would continue wheeling herself past the waiting room. I later learned her name was Amber.

She looked thin in her paediatric Johnny gown. The oversize gown covered her full body leaving her feet exposed. She wore ankle-length terry slipper socks. There was a stuffed golden teddy bear wearing a blue t-shirt laying on the left side of her thigh, almost tipping off. The t-shirt on the bear had the words "Foothills Children's Hospital".

She had bushy eyebrows and the most captivating huge green eyes that reminded me of Disney's Rapunzel's eyes. Her long black ringlets of hair covered half her face and contrasted with her ivory skin. She looked happy. I couldn't fathom why, considering the place we were in. Amber had a red lollipop in her mouth. Taking it out to speak, I noticed the colour had stained her pink tongue red. Her voice grated on me like a dentist's drill, that buzz deep in my brain. But to others from a distance, she may have sounded fruity-sweet and appealing.

"What's your name?" she asked, annoyingly breaking my reverie, as she slowed down right in front of me.

"My name is Harriet," I answered reluctantly, hoping my irritated tone would scare her away. That didn't stop her.

"I am Amber and I am nine years old. What are you doing here?" she asked.

One of those children oblivious to my derisive adult tone meant to send her away, she looked at me expectantly. "I'm here for physical therapy for my leg," I responded and this time did my best to scowl in addition to my "go away" tone. I just wanted to be left alone to my own misery.

"You have crutches. What happened to you?" Amber then asked, undeterred.

She was so annoying, persistent and obviously was sticking to me. I had to pay attention. I rewound the story of bitterness that played over and over in my brain.

My Trauma

I was a young teen, standing at 5'8" and weighing 110 pounds, working as a runway model. It was a cutthroat industry. I learned to embrace rejection. The experience ranged from harsh criticisms, false flattery, starvation, magazine photoshoots, and fashion week tributes to cultural experiences from different countries. After spending over ten years in the modeling industry, I decided to get a formal education enrolling as a student at the University of Calgary. The university was three hours away from my family.

Though outwardly I was popular, inside, I felt alone and vulnerable. I made a few friends, among which, Martin was one of them. He was charming, clever, thickset, short, and older than me. He was an introvert with few friends. We spent more and more time together. He became fond of me but would get jealous of the times I spent with my other friends, showing me this other side of him. He was manipulative, bad-tempered, lonely, and bothersome. In his determination to isolate me from my friends, he demanded to know and even controlled my whereabouts. The stalking started. I became afraid for my safety. As recommended by the police, I got a Restraining Order against him. I thought it was over.

Late one night, close to midnight, I was so involved in my project that I lost track of time. I quickly packed up my books and walked home to my apartment building. When I got into the building, I walked into the elevator without looking inside as I was searching for my house keys.

The door closed and somebody grabbed my neck from behind. I froze in fear.

"You thought you could escape?" I recognized him... Martin. The secured building and restraining order meant nothing to him.

He squeezed my neck so tight I could barely breathe. I heard voices from the hallway. I tried to scream, but he turned me around and punched me in the stomach. He took out a butcher's knife from his pocket and brandished it wildly to silence me.

"You know that I am the only person who loves you unconditionally," he said.

I spit on his face. Shocked and angry, he sliced into my right middle finger. I started bleeding profusely. I screamed for help. He was getting distressed. Martin then confirmed that if I screamed one more time, I would be dead. He took his shoes and socks off. He then folded the socks into a ball and shoved them into my mouth. Mute, disgusted, I gagged.

The elevator opened, and I pushed myself away from him. I ran towards the back door. His heavy-set body slowed him down. I grabbed the knob and pounded on the window. Please, somebody hear me. I opened the door just as Martin caught up with me.

He kicked my back. I fell and started crawling as fast as I could. The paved parking lot gouged my exposed knees. Cut and bleeding, I ignored the pain. Martin jumped on my legs and started hammering on my spine. I collapsed onto my stomach.

He turned me around, slapped me, and spit on my face. My head started throbbing. I trembled. I was speechless out of fear. I felt completely helpless, broken and ashamed. He wanted to have power over me. He tormented me by saying his actions were my fault. He blamed me for everything.

He pounded my head and stuffed me into the passenger seat of his car so he could control me. Ignoring stop signs and speed limits, crazed, he drove to a car dealership. He stopped and retrieved a baseball bat from the back seat. He proceeded towards the new cars and smashed their windshields, one by one. I was shaking uncontrollably, and my fingers and knees were throbbing in pain. I wanted to escape. What if I ran and he caught me again?

Martin returned, looked at me angrily and threateningly stated, "If you don't listen to me from now on, I will smash you like those windshields." We drove off to an isolated area in the middle of the bush. Neither one of us had a phone. He saw an emergency phone and ordered me to walk towards it and call my parents. The call was going to be my final goodbye to them because they would never see me again. I refused, and in anger, he told me, "I have a rope, a knife, a gun, and some gasoline. I am going to tie your body with the rope, cut you in pieces, and soak the pieces of you in gasoline, and no one will ever find your body."

Reaching for a thread of dignity, I trembled. "I don't care. If you love me, you won't hurt me like this," I cried.

"Love is listening, and right now, you are not doing that," Martin replied in anger.

He reached over my lap, opened the glove compartment, and took out what seemed to be a large hunting knife. This one was even bigger than the one he used to cut my finger.

Without another word, or hesitation, he raised the knife as high as he could and stabbed my left thigh twice. The blood immediately spurted out to the windshield. I lost consciousness. The next thing I remembered, I was waking up at the emergency ward at Foothills Hospital in Calgary. The doctor stated that I was lucky to be alive.

The media, police, and my father were all in the hospital waiting room. My anxious and worried father had driven for three hours that night, to be by my bedside.

Reading the news, I felt this was all my fault and how dare I bring shame to my family like this.

My Healing Process

I was horrified to be on crutches and having to learn to walk again. Once a runaway model, now a cripple. It just didn't make sense and my mind couldn't cope or accept any of this.

Additionally, the courts gave my abuser only three months in jail. I was outraged with the judge's decision to give him such a lenient sentence for attempted murder. I fell into a deep depression. I would cry silently, with no one to help. I was an embarrassment and failure to everyone in my life. Determined to end it all, I bought a bottle of sleeping pills, took them, and went to sleep.

I woke up disoriented. Trying to end my life was another failure.

Amber, this persistent, unwavering child was more than she seemed. She wanted to know my story. I told her a sanitized version suitable for her ears. She then shared her story with me.

Amber was an only child whose parents were instantly killed when a drunk driver ran a red light and struck their vehicle. She would be confined to a wheelchair for the rest of her life. She was motherless, fatherless, and homeless. Yet, she was full of joy and happiness. Curious, I asked her why she exuded joy.

She looked at me with a sincere smile and whispered, "I am lucky to be alive. Now here's a challenge for you – you are alive too. Why don't you use your experience to make a difference in your world?"

OMG, I thought. She's so right – a nine-year-old who was so much smarter than me.

She was the catalyst for my turning point, my call to action.

My Fantastic Life

I needed to meet Amber to find my purpose. The trauma taught me that one cannot expect a perfect life but must appreciate moments of beauty interspersed among tragedy.

I have deliberately released any bitterness, anger, and sadness that Martin had caused me. The hardships made me stronger. I got a second chance, a new beginning.

I use my experiences to help others. They can learn from my experiences without having to go through what I went through. By accepting myself, I can now own my story. I describe my life journey as moving from tragic to magic. I found my purpose. Now I live a fantastic life.

Now here's your challenge, start reading and applying the 13 golden pearls. And check out our **Secrets to Living a Fantastic Life** Facebook page and share with us how your journey is going. Talk to you soon.

About the Metaphorical Golden Pearls

The word "metaphor" combines the Greek words "meta" (between) and "phero" (to carry) and generally means to transfer between, as in transferring the characteristics of one thing to another. A metaphor is a type of analogy and is one of many figures of speech used to draw comparisons between two disparate entities.

The series of books by Mark Victor Hansen and Jack Canfield entitled *Chicken Soup for the Soul* shows how effective a metaphor can be when used well.

The series title manages to compare an every day food, thought to have magical healing properties, with that most elusive of human entities, the soul. You can also tell it's such a fabulous metaphor by the very fact that it takes so long to explain what the comparison is and how the metaphor was created.

In this book, we refer to the "golden pearls" waiting to be discovered in order to be Living a Fantastic Life.

Golden pearls do exist in nature. They are rare, and the deeper the gold colour, the rarer they are. The rarest has a deep gold colour and is referred to as a 24k golden pearl. They are grown in the gold-lip variety of the Pinctada maxima, South Sea pearl oyster in Indonesia, and the Philippines. Their warm, golden tones are completely natural, and no treatments are needed to enjoy the beauty of these gems.

Pearls are a perfect metaphor for transcendence.

Do you know how pearls are formed? When a foreign substance slips into the oyster, it irritates the shell and its organ. From that irritation, a tantalizing, mesmerizing, exquisite pearl is formed.

We invite you to be the judge of how they are the perfect metaphor for the transformations that Harriet and I have both accomplished.

GOLDEN PEARL #1

LOVE

Love – I believe that dreaming is stronger than reality. Desire is more potent than apathy. Hope is more powerful than despair. Joy always triumphs over sorrow. That laughter is the ultimate cure for mankind's foibles. And I believe that love is stronger than hate, the greatest gift of all. How do I know? I have been fortunate to experience them all. - Dr. Allen Lycka

The Shoe Box

There once was a little three-year-old girl who was extremely happy. She had angelic, curly red hair. She was always singing and playing. She never walked, she skipped everywhere she went. The world was her oyster. From sun up to sun down, everyone who saw her had a smile on their face.

One day, her father punished his three-year-old daughter for wasting a roll of gold wrapping paper. Money was tight, and he became infuriated when the child tried to decorate a shoebox to put under the Christmas tree.

Nevertheless, the little girl brought the gift to her father the next morning and said, "This is for you, Daddy."

The man became embarrassed by his overreaction earlier, but his rage intensified when he confirmed the package was empty when he unwrapped it. He yelled at her, "Don't you know that when you give someone a present, there is supposed to be something inside?"

"Oh, Daddy, you're so silly. It's not empty at all. I blew kisses into the shoebox. They're all for you, Daddy."

The father was crushed. He put his arms around his little girl, and he begged for her forgiveness.

Only a short time later, a tragic car accident took the life of the little girl.

Her father kept the gold-wrapped shoebox by his bed for many years, and whenever he was discouraged, he would take out an imaginary kiss and remember the love of the child who had put it there. And when he closed his eyes, he could see his little girl. He could even hear her giggle and feel her on his lap. He actually felt her kisses, and in his mind, felt she was still there with him.

Many years later, the man died of a broken heart. He went to heaven and St. Peter met him at the Pearly Gates.

St. Peter said, "To enter, you must give me something very valuable. I can't just let anyone in."

The old man gave St. Peter the most important thing he owned – the empty shoebox.

St. Peter smiled and said, "Enter my friend. You have given me the gift of everlasting love, the most valuable gift of all."

And inside, he was reunited with his precious daughter. She smiled at him and gave him a real kiss.

"I missed you," said the old man.

"Why, Daddy?" asked the little girl. "I never left you. When I died, God made me into an angel. When you opened the shoebox to get a kiss, I gave you one. I giggled in your ear, and I sat on your lap. I was always with you. I will always be your little girl."

- *Author unknown*

Moral of the story

"You always gain by giving love."
— Reese Witherspoon

Harriet: That's profound. But what makes you a love expert?

Dr. Lycka: Oh you - nothing in particular - just living. This is one of my favorite love stories. It reminds me that love is very complex. Did you know that according to the ancient Greeks, there are seven types of love?

Harriet: No way!!!

Dr. Lycka: Love, according to the ancient Greeks, was divided into seven types:

1. Eros – named after the Greek god of love and fertility romantic love
2. Philia – Affectionate Brotherly love
3. Storge – Familiar love
4. Mania – Obsessive love
5. Pragma – Enduring love
6. Philautia – Self-love
7. Agape – Selfless Love

Harriet: Wow – that's a lot to digest. It's all Greek to me.

Dr. Lycka: Haha. Yes, it is very hard to comprehend at first glance. But let's talk a little about each one, and I promise it will get easier.

Harriet: Great; I would love to know more.

Dr. Lycka: The ancient Greeks would have been upset by our use of one word to state, "I love you" and the same word to nonchalantly sign a letter with "lots of love." That wouldn't make sense to them. The types of love were and are distinct entities.

So, let's talk about Eros, the first type of love they acknowledge. Eros was named after the Greek god of fertility, and it signified sexual love. Maybe in today's language, it means "love-making." But the Greeks didn't always think of it as something positive because Eros involved losing control, and that frightened them. To them, it was wild and crazy love.

Harriet: That is odd because losing control is precisely what many people now seek in a relationship.

Don't we all hope to fall 'madly' in love? Love is irrational, out of control and that's viewed as bad in love. I was the victim of that mania when obsession took over. He was 'out of control'. His love was a form of madness like Cupid's arrows. I was oblivious to his intentions until his obsession forced me to open my eyes to a love that threatened my life.

Dr. Lycka: I know. True love means a lot of sharing and caring. But Eros is really about irrational or 'passionate love'. In your situation, your tormentor lost it.

That's why the Greeks valued the second type of love much more. It's called *Philia*, or the love that shows in a deep friendship such as that which is developed between brothers in arms who fought side by side on the battlefield. It was about showing loyalty to friends, sacrificing for them, and sharing their emotions with them. It involves love for fellow humans as well as care, respect, and compassion for people in need.

> *"Believe in love. Believe in magic. Hell, believe in Santa Claus. Believe in others. Believe in yourself. Believe in your dreams. If you don't, who will?"*
> *— Jon Bon Jovi*

Harriet: That's insightful. How much of this type of love do we have in our everyday lives. Our attempts to collect so-called 'friends' on Facebook or 'followers' on Twitter and Instagram – would have hardly impressed the Greeks. They don't impress me, either.

Dr. Lycka: Exactly. I think about the drama that goes on when someone unfriends someone else. Compare that to *Philia*, which is a 'profound love', not a superficial friendship.

> *My favorite thing in life is writing about life, specifically the parts of life concerning love. Because, as far as I'm concerned, love is absolutely everything. – Taylor Swift*

The third type of love is *Storge* (pronounced stor-JAY), a Greek word that means family love—the bond that is shared among family members. It encompasses the mutual love of parents and children. It has many of the characteristics of *Philia* but is not earned. It is natural.

Harriet: It seems to me that most families don't currently have enough *Storge*. I wish they did. My work at women's shelters shows me we need more *Storge*. That is my wish for the world.

Dr. Lycka: That's a deep thought. I could only imagine a world like that.

But the Greeks were smart. And for every yin, they recognized a yang. They saw a playful love they called *Ludus*. We've all experienced *Ludus* in the flirting and teasing during the early stages of a relationship. You can read about it in any Harlequin romance novel. But we also live out our *Ludus* when we banter and laugh with friends at a bar.

Harriet: *Ludus,* playful love. I think friends have fun being child-like too. We must remember to not lose the child within who loves to play.

I think that's why we are great friends.

Dr. Lycka: You gotta be kidding Harriet. I never joke. It's not in my manner.

Harriet: Yeah, right. What about the time when we were driving in Vancouver to get to the Miss World's contest.

Dr. Lycka: You mean the time we got lost? And your GPS kept taking us in circles and we almost ended up in Seattle?

Harriet: Yup. Good thing we had a full tank of gas.

Dr. Lycka: We are going to have to rename you, 'wrong way' Harriet.

Harriet: The name would be appropriate. I've been known to run marathons the wrong way.

Dr. Lycka: Ha, ha, now that name's definitely appropriate. Let's plow on. One of the higher types of love is *agape* or selfless love – a love that you extend to all people, whether family members or distant strangers. *Agape* translated into Latin as Caritas, which is the origin of our word "charity."

Harriet: In Edmonton, we have a Caritas Foundation that oversees a few hospitals. I believe in charity and giving.

Dr. Lycka: So do I. C.S. Lewis referred to charity as 'gift love', the highest form of Christian love. But it also appears in other religious traditions such as the idea of mettāor 'universal loving-kindness' in Theravāda Buddhism. I also think it is altruistic love and shown by selfless giving.

Harriet: I'm afraid agape is in a dangerous decline in many countries. Empathy levels in Canada and the U.S., in my opinion, have declined sharply over the past 40 years, with the steepest fall occurring in the past decade. We urgently need to revive our capacity to care about strangers. We need agape.

Dr. Lycka: I agree. We show this when we teach and volunteer. That's why we are speaking right now and sharing our thoughts with others.

And it's the simplest way to increase your love – give without thinking about getting.

So, agape is a bit like Christmas when it is better to give than receive.

Harriet: Are there other types of love?

Dr. Lycka: Yes – two others. The use of the ancient Greek root *pragma* as a form of love was popularized by the Canadian sociologist John Allen Lee in the 1970s who described it as a mature, genuine love that is commonly found in long-established relationships. Pragma is about making concessions to help the relationship work and showing persistence and open-mindedness. I don't think this was ever referred to in ancient Greek literature as a unique entity, but it was assumed. So, it is best considered as a modern update on the ancient Greek types of love.

I have found the paradox for that:

"If you love until it hurts, there can be no more hurt, only more love." – Mother Teresa

And then there's Philautia, or love of one's self:

The clever Greeks, such as Aristotle, realized there were two types of Philautia. One was an unhealthy variety associated with narcissism, where you became self-obsessed and focused on personal fame and fortune. A healthier version enhanced your wider capacity to love.

The concept is that if you love yourself and feel good about yourself, you will have plenty of love to give others (as is reflected in the Buddhist-inspired concept of "self-compassion.") If you fill your bucket, you have more to give and in that, there is a responsibility to take care of yourself.

Love is a force more formidable than any other. It is invisible – it cannot be seen or measured, yet it is powerful enough to transform you in a moment and offer you more joy than any material possession could.
– Barbara De Angelis, New York Times Best Selling Author

Harriet: In my volunteering, I have found that if a person had a mother or father who didn't love them, that person has a huge obstacle to overcome. They often cannot express love. They live in a shell, a bubble.

I initially gave those individuals four simple techniques to express love:

• Be patient with themselves.

• Surround themselves with people who love and support them now.

• Lose themselves in the service of others by volunteering. Doing so helps them value themselves because they can see the difference they are making to others.

• Exercise and meditate for the body, mind and soul. Use affirmations in their daily ritual, for example, 'I am enough', and 'I am worthy of Love'.

Dr. Lycka: No doubt, many things enhance love.

Harriet: Time for a knock, knock joke told to me by my daughter this morning.

Knock, knock!

Dr. Lycka: Who's there?

Harriet: Wiccan.

Dr. Lycka: Wiccan who?

Harriet; Wiccan figure it out, together.

Dr. Lycka: Groan. Now let's back on track.

As a doctor, I have also found some people literally cannot love, and it's often because some experience of needing love was missing or some other childhood experience such as bullying.

Harriet: Great minds think alike. I work with a group of young women in an organization I established, called *Empowered Me.* Some of the students who participate in the program have a strong emotional need caused by childhood deprivation and are incapable of loving. Most have issues with their parents/caregivers.

If the parents raise children in a loving environment, the impact has an ongoing positive effect on the child. If not, the child often suffers from emotional hunger and confuses other things for love. They try to find ways to fill in that void or emptiness and often repeat the unloving experiences that started it all.

Dr. Lycka: How do you teach them to love?

Harriet: I think you are trying to steal all my secrets, Doc Lycka. Shame on you.

No, this is an art, not a science. The first step is forgiveness. Holding onto hate is like trying to harm someone by drinking the poison yourself. Later in this book, we will talk about this some more.

Dr. Lycka: That's profound. It does, however, bring up another question. I'm sure many of our readers would like to learn how they can love more deeply.

Harriet: You already mentioned this. Love is one of the few things that increase in value when you give it away. You increase and intensify love by giving more. And the love must be unconditional. But it must be reciprocated from the person you are giving it to. Otherwise, unrequited love only leads to an empty relationship.

Dr. Lycka: This is where I need to mention a dear friend David Martz. His love reached out and touched me from Colorado Springs, Colorado to Edmonton, Alberta. It's because of it, I'm here today. But love is not a very logical thing.

Harriet: And I need to mention something. I still think you were trying to steal my thunder.

Dr. Lycka: I was. You caught me. I'm sorry.

Harriet: Don't let it happen again.

Dr. Lycka: But I will get the last word in. I believe Love is the greatest gift of all.

Harriet: No, you won't. I believe it as well. I get the last word.

> *"And in the end, the love you take is equal to the love you make." – Paul McCartney*

GOLDEN PEARL #2

INSPIRATION

Inspire – Live an inspired life. Be 'the inspiration' for someone else. Accept the inspiration given to you. - Harriet Tinka

The Little Girl That Could

A little girl sat on the ground visibly upset.

"What's wrong," asked her dad.

"I will never get this. Tying shoes is too hard."

"It is, *ma belle fille*. But nothing is too hard for my girl."

"Thanks dad. I will try."

She tried over and over, failing each time.

"Take a break. It will come," said dad.

She had a drink of water and tried again. "I think I can," she said.

She tried over and over. She kept repeating to herself "I ---think ---I can. I ---think ---I--- can. I ---think--- I ---can."

Then it became bedtime. "Time to sleep *ma belle fille.*"

Throughout the night the dad heard his daughter say,

"I think I can. I----- think-----I-----can.

I -----think----- I----- can."

Over and over again he could hear,

"I -------think --------I-------can."

The next day, the little girl tried again "I ---------think I can."

"Let's go to the store," said dad.

They found a doll with laces that could be tied. The little girl began trying to tie those laces.

"I ----think---I--can."

Over and over

"I ------think------- I------ can." Then it happened. She tied the laces.

"I----- thought------I-------could I----- thought----- I----- could. I thought I could. I thought I could. I thought I could."

And singing in victory, she hugged her dad.

- Dr. Allen Lycka

Moral of the Story: Inspiration comes from within

Dr. Lycka: My daughter's story is similar to the famous little engine that could. It was real for us. It is a story of true inspiration. If the little engine could do it, anyone could.

Harriet: Yes. I read that story to my children.

Dr. Lycka: As did I. Now, they read it to their children.

Harriet: I like the word inspire. Why? A life without inspiration cannot be lived. I love to run death races and ultra-marathons. The last one I ran was in Phoenix – barefoot – and I did my personal best. My inspiration drove me to want to do better. I also call it my passion.

> *"In life you need either inspiration or desperation."– Tony Robbins*

Dr. Lycka: Inspire. This word can be traced back to the Latin inspirare ("to breathe or blow into"), which itself is from the word spirare, meaning 'to breathe'. The earliest English uses of inspire give it the meaning "to influence, move, or guide (as to speech or action) through a divine or supernatural agency or power."

Harriet: What inspires you, Dr. Lycka?

Dr. Lycka: I look for people who have achieved great things and overcome adversity. Some of these are immortalized in movies.

One of my all-time favorites is *Chariots of Fire*. It tells the fact-based story of two athletes in the 1924 Olympics, Eric Liddell, a devout Scottish Christian who runs for the glory of God, and Harold Abrahams, an English Jew who runs to overcome prejudice. It's the story of a group of athletes who overcome tremendous odds to win the Olympics.

Another movie I love is *The Darkest Hour*. Set in May 1940, it is about the early days of Winston Churchill as Prime Minister. Nazi Germany's army began a blitzkrieg across Western Europe and threatened the UK. The German advance led to infighting throughout the highest levels of government between those who would make a peace treaty with Hitler, and Churchill, who refused. It's the story of perseverance and the ability to persist undefeated in the face of adversity.

One of my favourite inspirational people is Brendon Burchard. He is a three-time New York Times bestselling author and one of the best-known personal development trainers. He was in a devastating car accident, but this event did not destroy him. Instead, it launched him to an inspirational career, helping millions.

> *"People think, 'If I could only get motivated, then I'll act.' Nope. In actuality, it's the opposite." – Brendon Burchard*

Who are some of yours?

Harriet: I really like Mary Tyler Moore and Maya Angelou. They stood up for what they believed in. Here's one of my favorite quotes from Mary Tyler Moore:

> *"Success is liking yourself, liking*
> *what you do and liking how you do it."*
> *– Mary Tyler Moore*

And one of my favorite Angelou quotes is:

> *"My great hope is to laugh as much as I cry; to get my work*
> *done and try to love somebody and have the courage to*
> *accept the love in return." – Maya Angelou*

The Mary Tyler Moore Show is my favorite show because the theme song asks, "How will you make it on your own?" Mary Tyler Moore was a role model who inspired young, single women. She sent out the message that "you are going to make it after all," by making the impossible possible. She had a way of inviting women to not be afraid of making mistakes and be authentic by just being themselves. Moore's character told the audience that one has to fail to be brave. She encouraged women to accept themselves and enjoy their own company. Her role as a woman in broadcasting during that era validated that anything is possible if you work hard. She inspired me to do great things. Now I know that if I fail, I just have to get up and start again until I get it right.

Two of my favorite books are:

• Michelle Obama's *Becoming* and,

• *Malala,* a book by Malala Yousafzai, a young Afghanistan girl who stood up for education. As a result, she was shot by the Taliban. Taliban are defined as a brutal fundamentalist religious group.

And I would be remiss not to mention Amber who awoke me from my depths of despair.

Mmm... but I have one more. But I don't want it to go to your head. It's you, Dr. Lycka.

Dr. Lycka: You're kidding! I think you just want to butter me up.

Harriet: It's true.

Dr. Lycka: Thank you. I am honoured. And I must admit, you inspire me with every Ultramarathon and Death race you run.

Harriet: Thank you. What else inspires you?

Dr. Lycka: I've been passionate about helping people all my life. I have also been an advocate for women, especially in our male-dominated society. For many years, I sponsored the YWCA's 'Women of Distinction' in Edmonton, an organization that empowers girls and women and promotes peace, freedom, and dignity for all.

As a physician, I have removed tattoos for free from gang members and prostitutes to liberate them from the bondage of the streets. Survivors of terrible accidents received help with scar removal. A life renewed for many. I believe firmly in giving back. As they succeed, I am inspired.

Harriet: That shows your heart. And I remember the 'Women of Distinction'. That's where I met you, and I won for the category in which I was nominated – Turning Point!

Dr. Lycka: There you are back to winning – again.

Harriet: I always have a winning attitude and helps me stay strong and strive to do the best in everything I do.

"There is no passion to be found playing small – in settling for a life that is less than the one you are capable of living."
– Nelson Mandela

GOLDEN PEARL #3

VICTORY

"There is winning and there is misery." – Bill Parcells

Seabiscuit – What it Takes to Win

In the horse racing world, there are a few legends – Secretariat, War Admiral, Man o' War. But none tops Seabiscuit. Seabiscuit did not look or act like a racehorse. Born in 1933, he faced racing in the great depression. He dropped the first 17 starts of his career, leaving him as the butt of bad jokes in his own barn. But, as an article published on April 27, 1940, in the *Saturday Evening Post* read: "Seabiscuit is the Horatio Alger hero of the turf, the horse that came up from nothing but his own courage and will to win."

His strength? When he was in the post position, he couldn't bear to lose, especially when he was running second. He pulled out all stops to beat the opponent. That put him in the running for the greatest horse in the history of racing.

In 1937, Seabiscuit won 11 of his 15 races and was the year's leading money winner in the United States. In six seasons (1935–40) he won 33 of 89 races and a total of $437,730, a record for American Thoroughbreds (broken 1942).

The racing horse was known for his floundering stride, runtish tail, and thickset legs. In more ways than one, Seabiscuit represented the way that the U.S. was during the Great Depression. After recovering from his awful slump, Seabiscuit began winning races against every heavily favoured competitor.

Based on the movie *Seabiscuit*, a 2003 sport drama.

Moral of the Story – Our struggles in life develop our strengths and victories.

Dr. Lycka: Without struggles, we never grow and never get stronger. It's important for us to tackle challenges on our own and not rely only on help from others.

Accepting our own vulnerability sets us up for both success and failure. When we face our own vulnerability, we can accept the risks of reaching for success. Being vulnerable is neither bad nor good, but without it, victory cannot be achieved.

Harriet: Wow! What inspiration for an ultra-marathon runner such as myself.

Dr. Lycka: What's an ultra-marathon runner?

Harriet: The word marathon came from the Greek soldier Pheidippides's hometown. In 490 BC, he ran from his hometown called Marathon to Athens to deliver the news of victory over Persia. The distance was 25 miles away, and legend has it that he ran all the way there, delivered the news and dropped dead right on the spot. Any distance longer than 50 kilometres is now called an ultra-marathon. I usually run 125 kilometres barefoot and finish under 22 hours.

Dr. Lycka: What quotes inspire you when you are running?

Harriet: My favorite quote is by David Goggins, author of the book, *Can't Hurt Me.* "Two things that are inevitable about life - pain and suffering! No matter if you were born on third base having the world gifted to you, there's still no way to avoid it. If you can't imagine it, you better create someone that can! Attitude is absolutely everything in life! The only thing more contagious than a good attitude is a bad one."

What does racing teach me about winning? It is about courage and nurturing. It is about friendship. Winning is not a 'me' thing; it is a together thing.

It is hard to explain the feeling I have when I run – the inner satisfaction of knowing I have done my best. Being victorious is the result. I will never forget that fantastic feeling.

> *"Winning is the most important thing in my life, after breathing. Breathing first, winning next."*
> *– George Steinbrenner*

Dr. Lycka: So how do you win?

Harriet: Believe it or not, I have a formula.

Dr. Lycka: I knew it. You're organized.

Harriet: You have to be organized to be victorious.

> *"Nothing is black-and-white, except for winning and losing, and maybe that's why people gravitate to that so much."*
> *– Steve Nash*

Dr. Lycka: I would think it starts with setting specific goals.

Harriet: You bet. For example, when I run, I need to know where the finish line is. I've been known to fall down hills then run in the wrong direction.

Dr. Lycka: I could picture that.

Harriet: It's not a pretty sight.

Dr. Lycka: How do you overcome those moments?

Harriet: You can't blame others for your mistakes and you can't use excuses. Winners are people that are self-aware about their own mistakes, and they understand that it's their choices and decisions that brought them there. Winners don't use excuses; they find solutions.

Dr. Lycka: I know you are successful because you make winning a habit. And you're not afraid to fail.

Harriet: Taking risks and staying focused is important.

Dr. Lycka: Success rituals are too. What are yours?

Harriet: I wake up every day at 5 AM. That's the best time of the day as there is silence. I make the day count by starting my day with gratitude and a prayer for guidance. I will not look at my cell phone screen for an hour. I look outside to appreciate nature and see what to expect. Then off for a run, I go. I focus on what my seeds are for the day.

Dr. Lycka: Seeds are often best planted in the morning for the fruit that will grow later in the day.

Harriet: That's a great vision.

Dr. Lycka: Of course, I said it :)

"Winning is not a sometime thing; it's an all time thing. You don't win once in a while, you don't do things right once in a while, you do them right all the time. Winning is habit. Unfortunately, so is losing."
– Vince Lombardi

GOLDEN PEARL #4
VULNERABILITY

The Butterfly (Struggles)

A man found a cocoon of a butterfly.

One day, a small opening appeared. The man watched the butterfly for several hours as it struggled to force its body through that little hole.

Suddenly, the butterfly stopped making any progress and looked like it was stuck.

So, the man decided to help the butterfly. He used a pair of scissors to snip off the remaining bit of the cocoon. The butterfly then easily emerged, although it had a swollen body and small, shriveled wings.

The man didn't think anything of it and waited for the wings to enlarge to support the butterfly. But that didn't happen. The butterfly spent the rest of its life unable to fly, crawling around with tiny wings and a swollen body.

Despite his kind heart, the man didn't understand that the restricting cocoon and the struggle to get itself through the small opening were God's way of forcing fluid from the butterfly's body into its wings so it could fly once it was out of the cocoon.

- Author Unknown

Moral of the Story – Vulnerability allows us to struggle. Struggles build our strengths if we allow them and work through them.

Dr. Lycka: I'm going to say something that may upset you. It ties in with the last chapter – victory. But there is a more important word than victory. It's Vulnerable.

Harriet: Again, you're trying to steal my thunder. Vulnerability seems the opposite of being victorious.

Dr. Lycka: Actually, no. According to Brené Brown, a legendary vulnerability researcher, they come from the same place.

Harriet: How can they?

Dr. Lycka: At first, it sounds like they can't. They seem like opposites. But when you think about it and compare the two, they have the same foundation.

"Vulnerability is the birthplace of love, belonging, joy, courage, empathy, and creativity. It is the source of hope, empathy, accountability, and authenticity. If we want greater clarity in our purpose or deeper and more meaningful spiritual lives, vulnerability is the path."
– *Brené Brown,* Daring Greatly: How the Courage to Be Vulnerable Transforms the Way We Live, Love, Parent, and Lead

It's at the heart of winning, too. To go all out and win, you have to put it all on the line. You are very vulnerable.

We don't like vulnerability because we think it's bad; it's not. It's neither good nor bad. To win, you must take a risk. You must be vulnerable.

Let me ask a question. When you are putting it all on the line, trying to win, what are you?

Harriet: Vulnerable.

> *"Vulnerability is basically uncertainty, risk,*
> *and emotional exposure." – Brene Brown*

Dr. Lycka: Exactly. When you are trying to win, you allow yourself to be vulnerable. Because if you don't win, you lose, and you feel shame. We know and feel shame as very negative.

But, when you are willing to risk that to win, you are at your most vulnerable.

When I was in high school football for the Carol Cardinals, I played the tight-end. The quarterback called a play without a huddle. The coach sent in my buddy, Richard Brenner, to replace me and I immediately ran off the field in the middle of the play. On that play, we scored a touchdown that would have won the game. However, it was disallowed, because my leaving the field was deemed an illegal substitution. I wasn't knowledgeable of that rule, but still to this day, I carry the shame.

I learned a valuable lesson. I did my best with what I knew at the time. We played hard. Technically we won the game. When we learn to praise ourselves for the effort we put in, knowing we did our best, losing 'loses' the power to shame us.

> *"Victory is sweetest when you've known defeat."*
> *– Malcolm Forbes*

Harriet: I can see that when we are in win/lose scenarios. And I bet vulnerability also shows up when we bare all-important emotions – love, joy, and happiness. Being in love is a very vulnerable state. Being happy is vulnerable because happiness is fleeting. You must work at being happy. And joy is often replaced by sadness when life's events intervene.

Dr. Lycka: You got it. So are courage and creativity. Courage sounds like it is the opposite of vulnerability. But courage can only come out when one is very vulnerable. Creativity can also come out to play when one is willing to be vulnerable.

Writing is one of those things, too. What if you write a great book and no one reads it? That's the fear every writer has. And every great speaker. What if you stand at a podium, and everyone is searching for the bottom of Facebook on their phones? You fear worse than the proverbial rotten tomatoes being tossed – that they will ignore you. Worry is a very dark emotion that is driven by shame and fear of being shamed.

On the other hand, vulnerability is a positive driver. To not run a race because you fear you might lose is to run away from the very thing that gives the race purpose and meaning. And it's true about life in general.

When we reject vulnerability, we do so because we associate it with grief, sadness, and disappointment – all the things related to losing. But vulnerability is equally associated with winning and victory because if you never take a chance, you will never be victorious. You will never win. So, to win, you must be vulnerable.

Harriet: When I tell people of my weaknesses, I get a vulnerability hangover. Which means, I regret sharing my weakness. But, now I am beginning to realize it's a strength.

Wayne Gretzky, who many say was the greatest hockey player of all time, said, "You miss 100% of the shots you don't take." That means you must risk being vulnerable to be successful.

Let's go back to Brené Brown's quote that started this chapter. *"Vulnerability is the birthplace of love, belonging, joy, courage, and creativity. It is the source of hope, empathy, accountability and authenticity. If we want greater clarity in our purpose or deeper or more meaningful spiritual lives, vulnerability is the path."*

Dr. Lycka: Mother Teresa's quote adds to Brown's quote.

"Honesty and transparency make you vulnerable. Be honest and transparent anyway."– Mother Teresa

Harriet: I am not going to let you get the last word in. Yes, taking a risk, becoming vulnerable, makes you succeed. If you never take a chance, you can never win. But I still prefer winning to losing.

Dr. Lycka: We all do. But winning is a process, not a thing.

Harriet: Be quiet. I win. Nuff said.

Dr. Lycka: Ok, you win. But I get the last word.

Harriet: Hmmm. You always seem to.

Dr. Lycka: Of course. *Harriet mock pouts and I smirk.*

I guess I can't win even when I get the last word in.

Harriet gives even a bigger smile. "That's Girl Power," she says.

"I understand now that the vulnerability I've always felt is the greatest strength a person can have. You can't experience life without feeling life. What I've learned is that being vulnerable to somebody you love is not a weakness, it's a strength." – Elisabeth Shue

GOLDEN PEARL #5
INTENTION (PURPOSE)

"I work really hard at trying to see the big picture and not getting stuck in ego. I believe we're all put on this planet for a purpose, and we all have a different purpose... When you connect with that love and that compassion, that's when everything unfolds."
– Ellen DeGeneres

The Treasure

Once upon a time, there lived a wise man. He was the head of the local administration of a small village. Everyone respected him, and his views and opinions were well regarded. Many people came to him seeking advice.

His son, however, was very lazy and wasted his time sleeping and spending time with his friends. No amount of advice or threatening made any difference to him. He wouldn't change at all.

The years passed and with time faded the youth of the wise man. As he grew older, he began to worry about his son's future. He recognized the need to give something to his son so that he could take care of himself and his family to be.

One day, he called his son to his room and said, "My son, you are no more a kid now. You must learn to take responsibilities and understand life."

"I want you to find the real purpose of your life, and when you find it, remember it always, and you will lead a life full of happiness and joy."

Then he handed his son a bag. When the son opened the bag, he was surprised to see four pairs of clothes, one for each season. There was also some raw food, grains, lentils, a little money, and a map. His father continued, "I want you to go find a treasure. I have drawn a map of the place where the treasure is hidden. You need to go and find it."

The son loved this idea. The next day, he eagerly set out on a journey to find the treasure. He had to travel across borders, forests, plateaus, and mountains.

Days turned into weeks, and weeks turned into months. Along the way, he met a lot of people. Some helped him with food and some with shelter. He also came across thieves who tried to rob him.

Slowly the season changed, and so did the landscapes along with it. When the weather was unpleasant, he halted for the day and continued his journey when the weather cleared.

Finally, after a long year, he reached his destination. It was a cliff. The map showed the treasure placed below the cliff under the tree. Upon spotting the tree, he began to dig the ground. He searched and searched — around it, under it, on it - but found nothing. He spent two days looking and digging for the treasure. By the third day, he was so exhausted that he decided to leave.

Disappointed over his father's lie, he headed back to his home. On his way back, he experienced the same changing landscapes and seasons. This time, however, he halted to enjoy the blooming flowers in spring and the dancing birds in monsoon. He stayed in places just to watch the sunset in paradise or to enjoy pleasant summer evenings.

Since the supplies he carried were over by then, he learned to hunt and make arrangements for his meals. He also learned how to sew his clothes and shelter himself. He was now able to determine the hour of the day by the position of the sun and plan his journey accordingly. He also learned how to protect himself from wild animals.

He met the same people who had helped him earlier. This time he stayed a few days with them and helped them in some way or another to repay them. He realized how nice they were to an ordinary passerby who had nothing to offer to them in return.

When he reached home, he realized it had been two years since he left. He walked straight into his father's room.

"Father," he said.

"So how was your journey, my son? Did you find the treasure," he asked.

"The journey was fascinating, father. But forgive me for I wasn't able to find the treasure. Maybe somebody took it before me."

He surprised himself by what he just said. He wasn't angry at his father. Instead, he was asking for forgiveness.

"There wasn't any treasure in the first place, my son," his father answered smiling.

"But why did you send me to find it then," he asked.

"I will surely tell you why, in a minute, but first, you tell me, how was your journey to the place? Did you enjoy it?"

"Of course not, father! I had no time. I was worried someone else would find the treasure before I did. I was in a hurry to reach the cliff."

He continued, "But I did enjoy the journey on my way back home. I made many friends and witnessed miracles every day. I learned so many different skills and the art of survival. There was so much I learned that it made me forget the pain of not finding the treasure."

The father asked, "Did you find your purpose?"

The son looked perplexed.

The father said to him- "Exactly, my son. You want to lead your life with a goal. But if you remain too focused on the goal, then you will miss out on the real treasures of life. The truth is, life provides you with daily goals and you will find your purpose along the way."

- Author Unknown

Moral of the story

"Everybody has a purpose." – Dolly Parton

"The purpose of life is not to be happy. It is to be useful, to be honorable, to be compassionate, to have it make some difference that you have lived and lived well."
– Ralph Waldo Emerson

Harriet: This is my favorite chapter.

Dr. Lycka: Why?

Harriet: You ask the hard questions.

Dr. Lycka: It's my job, my purpose.

Harriet: And I think everyone needs such a purpose. The difficulty is finding that purpose.

In my work with youth and abused women, I find people have a hard time finding and living their intentions. They often misconstrue what they want and put themselves back into the same undesirable situation again. It becomes their 'groundhog's day'.

Dr. Lycka: I know the movie. *Groundhog Day* is a 1993 American comedy film. It stars Bill Murray, who plays Phil Connors, a TV weatherman. During an assignment covering the annual Groundhog Day event in Punxsutawney in western Pennsylvania, centering around a semi-mythical groundhog named Punxsutawney Phil, Murray is caught in a time loop. He repeatedly lives the same day.

Harriet: It's unfortunate, but many are caught in a *Groundhog Day* of their own making.

Dr. Lycka: So, how do you break out of a groundhog day life and discover your purpose?

Harriet: For you and me, it was going through life events that nearly killed us.

Dr. Lycka: The Japanese have two paths to learning: The path of pain (Kensho) and the path of insight (Satori). For us, our pain path gave us insight - Kensho became Satori.

And that gave us a purpose.

Dr. Lycka: Like my friend Jack Canfield, I am convinced everyone has a life purpose.

Look at our children. My oldest daughter is a nurse practitioner. My second is a stay-at-home mom and a massage therapist. My third is into public relations, and my fourth into home staging and yoga.

Harriet: My oldest son's passion is football. He tells me he was born to play ball. He loves it, he's good at it and he invests the time to be the best player. That's his purpose. My two girls are still finding their purpose.

I'm going to take some examples from my youth group and also from my volunteering with and supporting women fleeing domestic abuse.

My youth group and women often come to me, wanting me to help them find their purpose. We have all heard talks and quotes on purpose. They say, "Find what you are passionate about and run with it." The biggest thing is to work on whatever you are passionate about. If you love playing volleyball and you are passionate about it, what are you doing to master it? Invest in that passion. I tell them when the student is ready; the teacher will appear. They understand the proverb, but they want more lessons. To find their purpose, I share with them the concept of Ikigai.

Dr. Lycka: Sounds deep.

Harriet: You can take it at any level you want.

Ikigai (pronounced A-key-gay) is a Japanese concept that means 'a reason for being'. The word 'ikigai' is usually used to indicate the source of value in one's life or the things that make one's life worth-while (Wikipedia). The concept is based on asking yourself four questions:

1. Passion & Mission – What do you love?

2. Passion & Profession – What are you good at?

3. Mission & Vocation – What does the world need?

4. Profession & Vocation – What can you do and get paid for it?

I show the young girls and women that they cannot focus on one

purpose. Life is constantly changing as we move from one phase of our lives to the next.

When you are a student, your purpose is different; as a parent, your purpose changes again. We must remain open to more than our present purpose. Staying stuck is when we lose our path and therefore, our purpose. When my students can answer those four questions, they are on their path to finding their reason for being.

Dr. Lycka: Wow. Intention is really cause and effect. What you say and do should align.

Harriet: Let's explore how others can find a purpose. This is basically the legacy you leave behind. One essential key as we all go through the path of finding our purpose, is to let go of the ego. Tilopa was a scholar from the tenth century who stated, "Have a mind that is open to everything and attached to nothing." This means we have to see what is possible for us.

Dr. Lycka: Are you basically saying that we don't want to be self-absorbed?

Harriet: You bet. To find your purpose, this detachment is critical. Detachment is not that you own nothing; rather, it is that nothing owns you. Before you serve others, let go of the ego. How can we find a rudder to help our readers steer their boats?

Dr. Lycka: After you let go of the ego, evaluate the Things You Love To Do. We all have a hidden and profound intent that we must find. It is not something you need to make up or is given to you from someone else; it's already there. It is crucial to find it in order to have the life you want.

Harriet: Next, ask yourself, "What are you good at? Be honest with yourself. Are you good at listening to others? Is there a coaching career for you in the future?

What do you love to do?

This is not easy. Finding what resonates with you takes effort. But when found, it is self-evident.

Dr. Lycka: Effort is necessary for finding purpose, but misery is not required. If you are 'in pain', question as to whether you are living a life of purpose.

Harriet: How do you find your higher purpose?

"What is success? I think it is a mixture of having a flair for the thing that you are doing; knowing that it is not enough, that you have got to have hard work and a certain sense of purpose." – Margaret Thatcher

Dr. Lycka: Actually, it is there waiting for you. You have to uncover it. The next step is to ask what does the world need, and do I possess those qualities to close that needed gap?

Harriet: Here's a shortcut, first ask yourself, 'what' are two qualities I most enjoy expressing in the world? My two are persistence and caring.

Second, ask yourself, what are two ways I most enjoy expressing these qualities? My two are making an impact and giving people hope. We have a spiritual deficit, and the world needs someone to close this gap.

"Definiteness of purpose is the starting point of all achievement." – W. Clement Stone

I ignite and elevate people to rise up and let go of the negative beliefs with life-shifting stories. I do this through storytelling in my seminars, and I journal them in my books. I am most alive when I help transform teen's lives by teaching them to fall in love with themselves. It gives me meaning. Then these teens can love themselves unconditionally and make integrity-based decisions. I empower them by teaching them supercharged success strategies that they can apply in their own lives. It is critical to find what gives you meaning.

Dr. Lycka: The next question from the Ikigai Japanese concept is, "What can you do and get paid for it?"

Money can't buy happiness, but it is like oxygen. As our readers analyze this question, they should keep in mind that money will buy you a good time, but not peace of mind. Money will buy you a companion but certainly not a friend.

Harriet: It is important not to fall in love with money. But if your readers find Purpose/Intention they can get paid for, then Bingo! A new path is soon to come. Congratulations!

Dr. Lycka: We have both found our purpose and what gives us meaning. We do this by sharing our Golden Pearls of Wisdom. They are based on universal stories and the wisdom we discovered. I know I'll never become tired of them.

Harriet: Nor I. It's become our purpose, silly.

Dr. Lycka: I hope others can find their passion too. Here's a tool they can use. It's the passion test by Janet Bray Attwood. Go to the passiontest.com

Harriet: I did. It's a winner.

Dr. Lycka: Again, you try to get the last word in.

GOLDEN PEARL #6

NON-NEGOTIABLES

"The wise treat self-respect as non-negotiable, and will not trade it for health or wealth or anything else." – Thomas Szasz

The Secrets to Happiness

There once was a young man who wanted to learn about the secret of happiness from the wisest man on the earth. The lad wandered through the desert, mountains, and plains to find the wisest man in the land. He finally reached a beautiful castle high atop of a mountain where a very wise man was said to reside.

The young man had imagined the wise man to live like a sage with a modest and quiet lifestyle. But to his surprise, he was not at all like a sage. He saw lots of activities happening in the castle. Tradesmen came and went, people were conversing in the corners, a small orchestra was playing soft music, and finally he saw a table covered with platters of the most delicious food in this part of the world.

The wise man talked with everyone, and the young man had to wait for several hours to meet him. When he finally met him, the wise man listened attentively to know why the young man was so curious about the secret of happiness.

The wise man replied that he didn't have time to explain the secret of happiness at that moment. But he suggested the young man should have a look around his castle and its beauty and return in two hours.

He also assigned a task to the young man to carry out during the two hours. He handed the young man a teaspoon which had two drops of oil. The wise man said to the young lad, "As you wander around, carry this spoon with you without allowing the oil to spill."

The young man began climbing and descending the many stairways of the palace, keeping his eyes fixed on the spoon. After two hours, he returned to the room where the wise man was. "Well," asked the wise man, "Did you see the Persian embroideries that are hanging in my dining hall? Did you see the garden that took the master gardener ten years to create? Did you notice the beautiful parchments in the library?"

The boy was embarrassed and confessed that he had observed nothing. His only concern had been not to spill the oil that the wise man entrusted to him.

"Then go back and observe the marvels of my world," said the wise man. "You cannot trust a man if you know nothing about that man and his surroundings." Relieved, the boy picked up the spoon and returned to his exploration of the palace, this time more conscious about the surroundings and observing all the works of art on the ceilings and the walls. He saw the gardens, the mountains all around him, the beauty of the flowers, and the taste with which everything had been selected. Upon returning to the wise man, he explained in detail everything he had seen. "But where are the drops of oil, I entrusted to you?" asked the wise man.

Looking down to the spoon he held, the boy saw that the oil was gone. "Well, there is only one piece of advice I can give you," said the wisest man.

"The secret of happiness is to see all the marvels of the world, and never to forget the drops of oil on the spoon."

- *Author Unknown*

Moral of the Story – In everyone's life, there are non-negotiables that require our attention.

Dr. Lycka: I want to take a 'deep dive' into something I'm crazily passionate about.

Harriet: What's that?

Dr. Lycka: Everyone should have a list of principles they need to use as guideposts for their everyday living.

Harriet: I believe that too.

Dr. Lycka: I call them non-negotiables. I'm not sure where the principle came from, but it has become my cornerstone for business, life, and relationship for years.

> *"Non-negotiables are essential pearls of success. They are key to living. They define what you will never compromise on."*
> *– Dr. Allen Lycka*

Harriet: I know. I remember I was attending my second year of undergraduate university. My English Professor walked into class, handed out our new assignments and told all of us that the following ten requirements were non-negotiable. She listed them all and said that if we did not follow those guidelines, it would result in a failing grade or deduction.

Dr. Lycka: I am curious, what did she list for the students?

Harriet: I can't remember all ten. Just her top three:

1. Failure to cite details or quotes from sources would be an automatic fail.

2. Essays had to be a minimum of 1,000 words. If not, it meant a loss of one letter grade.

3. Essays had to be double spaced, or it was an automatic fail.

These requirements were non-negotiable. If I wanted to pass the course, I had to make sure I followed the requirements as the list was non-negotiable. Similar to you, that professor got me thinking about what aspects of my life were non-negotiable.

"Non-negotiables are a line in the sand."
– Harriet Tinka

Dr. Lycka: While we are on that subject, what are things in your life that are non-negotiable now?

Harriet: Dr. Lycka, you ask tough questions.

Dr. Lycka: Of course. That's the way I am.

Harriet: Haha. That's why we get along so well. You challenge me to think outside the box. This is what I have on my list:

1. Family

2. Respect

3. Honesty

4. Morals/ethics

5. Don't impact others with your choices (e.g., you decide to do drugs)

6. My value

7. Dignity

8. Health

9. Trust

10. Self-care

11. Work

Out of my list, my biggest non-negotiable is my value.

Dr. Lycka: They all seem important to me, but why do you choose 'my value' to be the biggest?

Harriet: It ties self-respect and self-confidence. I will share a story that convinced me that I should never compromise my value. But before I do, what is on your non-negotiable list?

Dr. Lycka:

1. Family/Friends

2. Work

3. Work

4. Work

5. Integrity

6. Health/ Exercise

7. Work, work, work

8. 13 golden pearls

Harriet: Hah, hah. You are a workaholic.

Dr. Lycka: No way.

Harriet: Yeah, right. But some of the things on your list are similar to mine. We are quite alike in many ways.

Here is that story I promised.

I was a teenager living in New York, working as a model. There were nights when I barely got enough sleep because my modelling schedule was so hectic. The industry was ruthless.

The expectations for models were clear. We were required to look thin and professional at all times. I remember my first photoshoot. I walked into the room nervously. I looked as helpless as a baby. My photographer introduced himself as Sebastian. He was 6'2", with long hair tied in a ponytail, green eyes, and a chiseled build.

I was impressed by how kind and patient he was with me. He photographed me and told me after the session that the raw pictures were outstanding. Raw meant they had not been edited for print work. I left feeling good about myself. I could not help thinking about Sebastian. He was handsome, and I thought about what he had said to me and how special I felt when I was being photographed.

The following day, the modeling agency looked at my pictures. One of the model scouts Jenny called me and told me over the phone, "Harriet, you are not thin enough, you need to be five pounds lighter. When you get to our target weight, Sebastian will shoot you for the next fashion campaign." All I heard from Jenny was "Sebastian." I was excited that I would see Sebastian again.

"Do not negotiate your dignity or freedoms; both are non-negotiable." – Mohammed Sekouty

I was a 'Fitting' model, which meant more pressure to be thinner than other models as designers used me as a live mannequin to fit their designs. I did what all the other models were doing to lose the weight quickly. I had to make sure I was thin enough to shoot in a week with Sebastian. I starved myself. I ate tissue papers to control my hunger pangs. Some days, I indulged by eating two grapes. For some of the models, having intravenous fluid administered in the hospital was part of being a supermodel. No matter what we did, it seemed, we were never good enough. But I didn't care; I wanted to get a chance to see Sebastian again.

A week later, the agency weighed me. I had lost 10 pounds. They told me how beautiful and thin I looked. I was ready to photograph with Sebastian. I walked into his photography studio. He had a display room of all the fashion models and campaigns he had done. I could hear Ludwig Van Beethoven, *The Fifth* playing in the background. I felt at ease and excited to be where Sebastian was. I wanted him to tell me how beautiful I looked. I was about to turn the pages of his portfolio when I heard his voice.

"Don't you look beautiful this afternoon, my lady. We will start shooting shortly."

My heart was beating fast, with wonderful emotions. I was in my glory.

My makeup artist and choreographer were in the room, and they chuckled at a distance. We started shooting with the Beethoven music in the background. It was magical. After four hours, we finished the session. I got my model's bag and started to walk towards the door when Sebastian held my hand and told me I was one of his best models.

The feeling I got from hearing that was un-measurable. I decided then, and there, I was going to do anything to impress him. That was my mission.

It was early September; New York Fashion week was scheduled. These were special invitation-only events. They were called the 'Big 4 Private Runway shows.' (Big 4 meant New York, London, Milan, and Paris). The New York one was Sebastian's favorite. He invited me to attend with him. I was going to be Cinderella at the Ball. We had a marvelous time. There began our relationship that would test my non-negotiable list.

We spent endless time together. From the Brooklyn Botanical Gardens, Central Park, Broadway shows, football games to picnics to cafes to people watching. It was romantic. He brought me so much joy.

"When we know what's essential in our lives, everything else is negotiable. What are some things you don't do? What things could you intentionally leave undone so that you can focus more deeply on the things you feel called to and passionate about?" – Shauna Niequist

Our schedules started getting busy. I was often traveling from city to city and working late. Our times together were beginning to be limited. We had been together for nine months. Sebastian was ten years older than me. He started telling me that I was gaining a lot of weight and that I needed to lose weight to have good fashion photos. I wanted to make him happy and decided to compromise my values to have his validation. He would exacerbate my fears and tell me I was not good enough. I did my best to please him. My modeling agency was also telling me I was not good enough.

I continued to model in an industry projecting unrealistic images of me. Women and girls were trying to fit into an image they would never sustain, and men were feeding into this story as well. I got emails from girls around the world, wishing that they looked like me. Suddenly it dawned on me, wait a minute: Harriet, you are not empowering these young girls and women. Quite the contrary, you are feeding into their low self-esteem. These girls, your fans, are indulged in endless internal dialogues of, "Oh no, I am not good enough." I was compromising my self-respect and value to please others.

One day I read a statement made by my favorite designer Karl Lagerfeld against a German magazine that used 'ordinary real' women rather than professional models. Lagerfeld claimed the world of fashion is about selling dreams and illusions, and people prefer to see skinny models, not fat-mothers who sit with their bags of potato chips in front of the TV.

When I read that, I said enough is enough – no more, no way. I was allowing the industry to destroy my self-esteem; I, as a participant, was destroying the self-esteem of your sister, your mother, your girlfriend, your daughter, your wife, your husband, your boyfriend, your brother. I relied on my fake images to validate myself. The industry stole my identity. I was ashamed of my look. But I wished to live my life without shame. I just didn't know what that looked like.

I ended the relationship with Sebastian. I then left the industry and started to work on myself. I focused on progress rather than perfection. I focused on how far I had come rather than how far I had left to go. I was determined to pave the way to empower young women and girls. And I was never again going to compromise myself to please others.

> *"Trust and truth are not negotiable."*
> *– Dr Allen Lycka*

If you are enough for yourself, you will be enough for others. Beauty begins when you decide to accept yourself. I was not going to compromise my self-respect or my value to stay in an industry that did not value me. In addition to all other things on my list above, those were my top non-negotiables. Just like my professor had a non-negotiable list for the assignment requirements, I have my own.

When you figure out your list of top five non-negotiables, the tough part is over, and now the next step is to ask yourself the following questions:

• Do my habits support my non-negotiable list?

• Do my friends align with my non-negotiable list?

• Do my thoughts align with my non-negotiable list?

If the answer is no to any of those questions, then there is work to be done to value yourself and not compromise your list.

> *"Beauty begins when you learn to love yourself."*
> *– Harriet Tinka*

Dr. Lycka: That's powerful. Life begins with non-negotiables. But it doesn't end there.

> *"Non-negotiables are the driving force for life."*
> *– Dr. Allen Lycka*

For me, a non-negotiable is work. For forty years, I have been a doctor and worked day and night at this. I have literally sweated blood. To say I am a workaholic is a mild statement.

I get more done by 10 AM than most people do in a week, maybe a month.

But my other non-negotiables are equally enlightening. Let's look at these:

• Family – nothing comes in the way of family; my wife, my daughters and their husbands, my grandchildren, etc. My wife has taught me work is not as important.

• Integrity – defined as 'the quality of being honest and having strong moral principles; moral uprightness'. I love to be known as 'a man of integrity'. My word is my bond.

• Recently, health has become a priority. I have had to concentrate on it because of life's events.

• But I would be remiss to not mention the '13 Golden Pearls'. Any and all are non-negotiable.

"Life is based on 13 golden pearls." – Harriet Tinka

Harriet: I was going to let you get the last word in. Not this time. I began this chapter with a quote:

Dr. Lycka: That's why the wise are wise, Harriet.

GOLDEN PEARL #7

FORGIVENESS

As we know, forgiveness of oneself is the hardest of all.
- Joan Baez

My Uncle

My mom and I walked side by side down the hospital hallway before the birds started to sing. I hadn't slept a wink the night before and I doubt she had either. We were trying to be strong for one another, but we were both drained. My dad, every breath laboured, was fighting for the next moment and the next. He was about to be transferred to a teaching hospital in the big city where multiple doctors would be on the case. As we approached his room, we saw something that made us pause. A man in a dark navy Armani suit stood by my father's bedside with his back to us. My mom turned to me and remarked, "Isn't it nice the doctor is here to see your dad so early?" Outside his hospital window, the light of day was just dawning over the edge of town.

As she turned from my ear, I noticed that the man was holding my dad's hand. And then for a moment, I felt like I was dreaming as I recognized his stance. "That's not a doctor." It was my father's brother. My dad and uncle, estranged, had not exchanged a word for as long as I could remember. I didn't know then, but our lives were about to be forever changed.

I never really understood why my dad and uncle had stopped speaking years before. I just knew that during family functions, no room or facility was ever big enough to smooth the tension in the air as they pretended the other wasn't there. Us cousins floated on the peripheries of our fathers unable to fully cross over lest we be seen as a defector. The rest of the family pretended normalcy, ignoring it was anything but. If we did talk about it, it was in hushed tones with harnessed curiosity and then buried again. It left its mark.

That day in the hospital and those that followed turned out to be some of the most difficult of my 19 years. My dad had had a brain aneurysm and needed to be in the Intensive Care Unit. It was a scary time for my mom and us, especially me as her main supporter, but after discovering my uncle by my dad's bed, he stayed with us through the whole ordeal. I had no appetite, nor mom but he brought us healthy snacks and made sure we ate them. He also let me use his cell phone (a novelty in those days) to call my best friend and distant siblings with updates about dad. When I think back on those hazy days in the ICU, the one thing I clearly recall is my uncle by our side the entire time.

I'm so very thankful to say that my dad ended up pulling through and did not even need to have surgery to correct the aneurysm. Somehow it healed itself while he was in the hospital, which always seemed like somewhat of a miracle to me. But the real miracle was that my father and my uncle were back together again. My dad couldn't be mad at his brother anymore. He hadn't just been there for him, but he had also been there for us. He got us through the hardest days of our lives, and none of us would ever forget that. My uncle's slate – wiped clean.

After my dad recovered, he and his brother became inseparable. It was my privilege to witness them filling in the gaps of the lost years and even be privy to some of those conversations and man cave time. They became closer than close. Family gatherings no longer had a dividing line. His wife and my mom sharing inside jokes over the stove and presiding over family meals. I had no idea friendships with cousins would become primary in my life. Eventually, after my dad retired from his career, he even went to work for his brother's business. And when I became pregnant with my son, my uncle created a job for me where I could work from home. Not having to leave my baby to go to work was a dream come true. He made it possible. It's truly one of the greatest gifts I received in my life.

Four years ago, we were devastated when my uncle died. How could we be robbed of this man when he was only 58? His passing has been such an incredible loss for our whole family. Though brokenhearted, my dad was there for his brother's wife and three grown sons, the same way my uncle had been there for my mom and us twenty years prior.

The packed church on the day of his funeral was a testament to the kind of man he was and the way he lived his life. I'm so thankful that our family is included in the tally of the lives he touched, made possible by the gift of forgiveness. The one thing I especially miss is seeing the two of them, heads bowed scheming jokes or planning the next best business move together. They always reminded me that all things are possible. Uncle if you are listening, I want you to know I have stored your lesson in a safe place and it serves to remind me whenever little irritations pop up, none of it matters more than love.

- Lauren

Moral of the Story – Forgiveness is the essence of love

Dr. Lycka: Let's talk about forgiveness.

Harriet: Psychologists generally define forgiveness as a conscious, deliberate decision to release feelings of resentment or vengeance toward a person or group who has harmed you, regardless of whether they deserve your forgiveness.

Dr. Lycka: One of the most powerful books on forgiveness ever written, is *"The Book of Forgiving,"* written by Archbishop Desmond Tutu along with his daughter, the Reverend Mpho Tutu. Together they offer a guidebook on the process of forgiveness—helping us to realize that we are all capable of recovery and healing.

Tutu's role as the Chair of the Truth and Reconciliation Commission of South Africa taught him much about forgiveness. What was universally predicted as inevitable in South Africa after apartheid was a bloodbath, where blacks attacked whites as a reprisal. Yet, instead, South Africa chose forgiveness and reconciliation.

"Forgiveness is not always easy. At times, it feels more painful than the wound we suffered, to forgive the one that inflicted it. And yet, there is no peace without forgiveness."
– Marianne Williamson

Harriet: Don't forget Viktor Frankl's *Man's Search for Meaning*. His story also reminds me forgiveness is a choice and true freedom comes from exercising that choice. Like Frankl, I have always found forgiveness to be even more important for the giver, not the receiver. Otherwise, we give up all our power to the other and remain a victim.

Dr. Lycka: I agree. To me, all hurting comes from pain, especially pain we hold onto. When we resist letting go, and indulge in thoughts or acts of revenge, retaliation, and hate, we keep the cycle going and going and…. I once read that forgiveness does NOT mean you have to break bread with the transgressor, what it does mean for you, in the most positive sense, is to wish them well and release, which corresponds to Tutu's teachings.

To Desmond and Mpho, the cycle is broken by a fourfold process:

1.   Telling the story,

2.   Naming the hurt,

3.   Granting forgiveness and

4.   Renewing or releasing the relationship.

"There would be no need for love if perfection were possible. Love arises from our imperfection, from our being different and always in need of the forgiveness, encouragement and that missing half of ourselves that we are searching for, as the Greek myth tells us, in order to complete ourselves."
– Eugene Kennedy

Harriet: Hate begets hate. It's a vicious cycle. We can choose to break the cycle with forgiveness.

"Darkness cannot drive out darkness; only light can do that. Hate cannot drive out hate; only love can do that."
– Martin Luther King

Dr. Lycka: Harriet you know that all too well.

Harriet: When I was viciously attacked, I could have easily chosen a path of hate. But that 9-year-old girl, Amber, showed me the path of love and forgiveness, not anger and despair.

Dr. Lycka: When I was a practicing dermatologist, I was an expert in scar correction. I was trained by the world's experts and made even the worst physical scars disappear.

Now I know how to make emotional scars vanish.

Here's another acronym: **SCARS**

S – Speak/ Say/ Spell

C – Comprehend

A – Assurance

R – Relinquish

S – Succeed

S – Speak/ Say/ Spell your hurt story out. You need to own your story. You can't suppress it. Take your time. Shout it out if necessary. Punch a punching bag, but get it out. Often, a person needs professional psychological help through this phase. Your journal pages can help too.

C - Comprehend why it happened. Mentally, most people cannot let it go until they know 'why'. Was the perpetrator evil? A narcissist? Were you in the wrong place at the wrong time like the victims of the Las Vegas shooting?

A - Awareness. Know in your heart of hearts it won't happen again if…. For many of us, repeating the lessons of life will continue until we look within. Assurance it won't happen again requires we find the lessons, clean our hindsight window to see the good and the sooner we do that, the more moments of life you can spend in a positive vibe. (See Eric Edmeades 'Hindsight Window' on Youtube.) Positive vibes attract more of the good stuff of life. Learning the lessons of the unpleasant interactions creates a new way to live assuring you are now aware of the wound that needed healing. You have now learned a new dance, no longer knowing the steps the perpetrator needs to match in order to waltz into your life.

R- Relinquish the pain and forgive the person who inflicted it. Remember – this is your right, your responsibility, your true power to reclaim and serves you far more than the doer of the wrongful deed. Let it go. You don't need it. It only holds you back. Freedom is a choice. It is your choice to make and a gift only you can unwrap.

S – Succeed. Don't look back. Move forward. Deepak Chopra says, "In any situation you have the choice of being a creator or a victim. Your success is tied up with your ability to empower yourself and tap into your innate creativity. That is where your power lives."

Harriet: I would like to emphasize, everyone and everything can be forgiven if you let it happen.

You know my university story, the dark days after I was left for dead. Viktor Frankl was starved, beaten, tormented. He is a model for choosing forgiveness and love. Letting it go was one of the most challenging things I have ever done. It wasn't quick either. Sadness lingered and negative thoughts and anger surfaced in me at the oddest times. For too long, I stayed stuck in the 'why did it happen to me?' mode. I questioned everything and felt consumed with hate and anger. Forgiveness is like a snake bite. The bite will never kill you; it's the venom. You must remove the venom from your veins before it destroys your heart. The snake was my abuser. The venom was my anger and resentment. It took time for me to understand that metaphor.

"Forgiveness is giving up the hope that the past could have been any different, it's accepting the past for what it was, and using this moment and this time to help yourself move forward." – Oprah Winfrey

One day my father came to my room, sat on my bed, and told me a Cherokee Indian legend about two wolves.

Dr. Lycka: I don't think I've ever heard it. Can you share the legend?

Harriet: Yes, I will, as it was another turning point in my path to forgiveness. In many ways, I had wished my past was different.

This is the story my father shared:

"An old Cherokee was teaching his grandson about life. His grandson had come to him with anger because a friend had done him an injustice.

The grandfather said to him, "I too have felt so much anger for those who have taken so much and have no sorrow for what they do. But hate wears you down and does not hurt your enemy. It's like drinking poison and wishing your enemy would die. I have struggled with these feelings myself. It is as if there are two wolves inside me.

One is good and does not take offense when offense is intended. He will only fight when it's right to do so and in the right way.

But the other one ugh...he is full of anger and hate. He fights everyone, every time, for no reason. He cannot think because his anger and hate are so great. It is helpless anger because his anger will change nothing.

Sometimes it is hard to live with these two wolves inside me. Both try to dominate my spirit."

The grandson thought about it for a minute and then asked his grandfather, "Which wolf will win?"

The old Cherokee simply replied, "If you feed them right, they both win. You see, if I only choose the White Wolf, the Black one will always be hiding, waiting for me to be distracted or weak and jump to get the attention he craves. He will always be angry and fight the White Wolf. But if I acknowledge him, he's happy, and the White Wolf is happy, and they both win. The Black Wolf has many qualities: tenacity, courage, fearless, strong will, and great strategic thinking that I need at times that the White Wolf lacks. But the White Wolf has compassion, caring, forgiveness, and the ability to recognize what is best for all. You see, son, the Black Wolf needs the White Wolf at his side. To feed only one would starve the other, and it would become uncontrollable. To feed them both means they will serve you well and do nothing that is not part of something greater, something good and something of life. Feed them both, and there will be no internal struggle for your attention. And when there is no battle inside, you can listen to the voices of deeper knowing that will guide you in choosing what is right in every circumstance. Peace, my son, is the Cherokee mission in life. A man or woman who has peace inside has everything. A man or woman who is pulled either way inside has nothing. How you choose to interact with the inner forces within you will determine your life."

That story gave me hope in understanding the Pearl of Forgiveness.

Dr. Lycka: That legend has lessons we can all learn from when forgiving. I was misdiagnosed as ALS. If I had listened, I would be dead. But I forgave the doctor who made the misdiagnosis.

There is nothing that cannot be forgiven.

Harriet: Except maybe you. You keep trying to get the last word in.

Dr. Lycka: Not me. It's not in my character. I'm not the black wolf.

Harriet: Yeah, right, I know better.

> *"Mistakes are always forgivable, if one has the courage to admit them."* — Bruce Lee

GOLDEN PEARL #8

ATTITUDE

"You play the hand you're dealt. I think the game's worthwhile." - Christopher Reeve

Afghanistan Story

Roya Shams was torn. This day, November 19, 2019, should have been 'the happiest day of her life.' It was her graduation day from the University of Ottawa with a degree in International Studies and Globalization. But she was sad because her father was not there to celebrate it with her.

Her father had been killed by the Taliban in 2011 after he challenged the Taliban's belief that women should not have an education. And after his death, Shams became a target of the Taliban. She received death threats and, as a result, she rarely left her home.

But her father's death was not in vain. A Toronto Star reporter, Paul Watson, heard of Raya Sham's plight and discussed the situation with editor Michael Cooke, who helped her to come to Canada – a long and arduous journey that brought her from the deserts of war-torn Kandahar to the classrooms of the University of Ottawa.

She was able to attend school because of the generosity of donations. She first attended high school at Ashbury College, which waived her tuition enabling her to attend. And she was able to attend the University of Ottawa with the help of $7,000 in donations raised by Toronto Star readers, and a scholarship from the University of Ottawa.

Shams' journey to this country, having no English skills upon landing on Canadian soil, required all the tenacity she could muster. The achievements she had gathered are due to this inner drive and a profound desire that makes success the only viable option. Inspired by her father, knowing one's life is a gift not to be wasted, she put in many arduous hours developing her proficiency in English, as her Afghanistan education left her far behind in the skills she would need in Canada. While other people would burn a candle at both ends, she knew she had to cut hers in the middle, dig out the wick, then depended on her inner reserves to burn the four ends to get the job done.

Now, as she extends her reach, she has her sights set on achieving another major milestone in life, she is thinking of others, especially other women in her native country.

"All I was thinking was for all those girls who are dreaming of such a day and can't have it," Shams told *Ottawa Morning* host Robyn Bresnahan.

"We girls need to hold each other's hands to be strong," Shams said to Sahar Fatima of the *Toronto Star*. "In the future, I'm hoping that even if one person could hold a hand and get taken out of the situation they are in, that would be a life accomplishment for me."

Her future plans are to attend law school to help women overcome laws that limit their ability.

"My intention is to do international human law, especially when it comes to women. I want to change lives for women back in Afghanistan, or any country where women are oppressed," she told Aron Hemens of *The Fulcrum*.

Moral of the Story – Attitude shapes your destiny.

Dr. Lycka: I want to share with you an essential element of success: it is attitude. I could attempt to say it again, but many years ago, Earl Nightingale wrote the definitive text on attitude. Rather than trying to recreate it poorly, I am going to include it here (with permission).

What word would you say is the most important word when it comes to living successfully? According to the experts, the word is 'attitude.' And it is a fact that our attitude will determine our fate and success. The dictionary defines attitude as, "A noun meaning position, disposition, or manner about a person or thing."

Your attitude clearly determines what happens to you in life. Your attitude determines whether or not you will enjoy it and finish it successfully. Similar to the reciprocal concept, "We get back measure for measure exactly what we put in." With regards to attitude, "We get back measure for measure an exact reflection of what we put out." Therefore, if you find people are reacting unfavorably or if you get the idea the world is picking on you - it might be time to look at the attitude you have been presenting to others and the world. Check your attitude!

You have a choice regardless of the circumstances to be either cheerful or not. There is absolutely nothing to be gained by being defensive, grumpy, or even mean - so why be it? If you develop the right attitude, you will find others will have the same positive attitude towards you. Things begin to go your way.

You start to feel lucky.

As Henry Chester once said, "Faith and initiative, rightly combined, remove mountainous barriers and achieve the unheard and miraculous. An enthusiastic attitude is nothing more than faith in action."

Be cheerful, positive, and determined - you will go far!
– Earl Nightingale

Harriet: That is amazing. I understand Earl spent his early years studying what it means to be successful. Attitude is truly one of the most important things you bring to any situation. It is a game-changer.

*"Being a sex symbol has to do with an attitude, not looks.
Most men think it's looks, most women know otherwise."*
– Kathleen Turner

Dr. Lycka: Nothing affects more aspects of your life than attitude. It changes the following interlocking spheres – your emotional state, your personality, your social interactions, your health, and your career.

Harriet: When you think about it, the impact of one's attitude is pretty overwhelming.

Dr. Lycka: It is but, it doesn't need to be. Go back to Earl Nightingale's five paragraphs. It's all there. It's simple.

*"Attitude is absolutely everything in life! The only thing
more contagious than a good attitude is a bad one."*
– David Goggins

Dr. Lycka: Let me share a little story. I had a teenage patient about 20 years ago. Like many teens, he was bothered by his acne. What was unusual, though, was that he was so bothered, he wouldn't go to school.

I talked to him at length, and he gradually came around. We started him on acne meds, which cured his acne.

He blossomed. He went on to complete a PhD from Harvard. Recently, he came to see me shortly after his mother died.

He was grateful. But more importantly than curing his acne was the change in his attitude. He was no longer the "ugly duckling." He mentally and physically transformed into a beautiful swan.

Harriet: Life circumstances must have changed his outlook in life. When we overthink matters, we complicate them.

We have to retrain our thinking and speaking into positive patterns if we want to change our lives. That's where affirmations come in. They replace the negative 'self-talk'.

An affirmation is something we say over and over, and it transforms who we think we are. Here are a few:

1. I am the architect of my life; I build its foundation and choose its contents.

2. Today, I am brimming with energy and overflowing with joy.

3. My body is healthy; my mind is brilliant; my soul is tranquil.

Dr. Lycka: Those mantras of self-care will foster a positive attitude.

Harriet: You nailed it. You mentioned earlier that attitude clearly determines what happens to you in life. The food you grow in the valley is the food you will find on top of the mountain. My student Jen came to me one day and told me that she understood what attitude was. She indicated that in her mind, it is being in a positive mental state. That wasn't her normal. She wanted to know how she could handle the negative side of attitude. She just didn't know how to deal with the diseases of attitude.

Dr. Lycka: We can talk about many diseases of attitude. The late Jim Rohn was an expert on the diseases of attitude.

Harriet: Indeed. But I often focus on the ones that have a big impact on individual students. This way, I can support their mental growth as they build their confidence and focus on an attitude of gratitude.

Dr. Lycka: For Jen, what did you focus on?

Harriet: Jen was notorious for having self-doubt, for worrying about everything and constantly complaining about life.

Dr. Lycka: That's a full package!

Harriet: I basically focused on each attitude-disease to help her sort it out. Self-doubt is an attitude-disease that is a risk factor for depression.

Symptoms are usually feelings of worthlessness and indecisiveness. Jen was guilty of undervaluing her abilities and contributions, which prevented her from realizing her full potential. Her inner critic would constantly ask, "What if I can't do it?" "What if people laugh at me?" "What if I fail?" "Am I good enough?" These were her inner critics protecting her. Our brains are hot-wired to place boundaries between us and the risk of failing. Our behavior will not deviate from our internal mapping.

When I hear my 'self-doubt voice', ask me, "What if I fail?" I tag that self-doubt voice; I then have an internal dialogue asking why I feel that way. Then I uninstall that voice. It must be deleted from my system because it's not adding any value to my temperament. I advised Jen, the next time she experienced a self-doubt dialogue, to tag it and uninstall it and use that mental rehearsal repeatedly. Self-doubt mindset is a habit and can be changed. I suggested to Jen to control the controllable.

"My attitude is that: if you push me towards something that you think is a weakness, then I will turn that perceived weakness into a strength." – Michael Jordan

My recommendations to Jen on how to cure this attitude-disease were to:

1.   Give herself credit for what she had done. The accomplishments she achieved were real and belonged to her. Own them and be proud of them.

2.   Believe in and not under-value herself.

3.   Surround herself with accountability partners/mentors who lift her up – people who can hold up her personality mirror to help her see what she doesn't see.

4.   Monitor her attitude to avoid falling into a depression.

Dr. Lycka: How about the attitude-disease of worrying?

Harriet: That one was a challenge. This attitude-disease can increase your blood pressure and, at high levels, lead to a heart attack or stroke.

Worrying kills performance, dreams, and enthusiasm. Some of us are professional worriers. This can be very crippling. The thought process often goes from exciting to being fearful and back to being excited again. It's a roller coaster. Worrying triggers those stress hormones that elevate your heart rate and breathing, similar to an anxiety attack. Negative thoughts are created, increasing additional stress.

Dr. Lycka: Bruce Lipton speaks to this. He asks: *"Well, what happens physiologically when we're experiencing fear in our mind?"* And the answer is, *"The brain releases elements such as stress hormones as cortisol or norepinephrine as well as agents that affect the immune system such as histamine or cytokines."* Like, *"Oh, so, what is the collective response of the chemistry of fear in the blood?"* And the answer is, *"It redirects the flow of energy in our body."*

Let's go on. What did you do next?

Harriet: I gave Jen some examples she could relate to, so she didn't feel like she was alone in the attitude-disease of worrying.

A friend presented an outstanding Request for Proposal document to a potential supplier. The response was to be announced within five business days. He had all the qualifications, background, skills they were looking for and even outlined the advantageous return on investment to the potential supplier. He spent the entire week worrying about the results. He could not sleep, and it became unbearable to be around him. Imagine what it did to his disposition. It was a good two weeks later when he found out the results. Unfortunately, his stress level was too high as he had not taken the time to look after his health and suffered a minor stroke. He has since recovered, but it was a lesson learned. Unnecessary worrying is destructive.

Dr. Lycka: Worry is useless energy.

Harriet: This attitude-disease rewires your brain to attract negativity. It increases your stress hormone and can cause weight gain, heart attack, or even a stroke. According to the Daily UK, we spend an average of eight minutes forty-six seconds a day complaining.

Jim Rohn provided a great visual in the following statement: *"Spend five minutes complaining, and you have wasted five, and you may have begun what's known as economic cancer of the bone. (If you complain), they will soon haul you off into a financial desert, and there let you choke on the dust of your own regret."*

Dr. Lycka: That is a profound description. We all know someone in our life who, no matter how great things are going, they will complain about something. They will complain, whine, frown and repeat.

Harriet: To say we should never complain is unrealistic. But explaining an issue, puzzle or challenging situation reasonably in a mature, problem-solving way to find the win-win is different.

Dr. Lycka: Can we overcome the tendency to complain?

Harriet: Yes. Here's my plan:

1. Concentrate on gratitude – Put things in perspective. Instead of focusing on what elements in your day did not turn out the way you like, write down the good things – even the small occurrences.

2. Use an elastic band around your wrist to make you aware when you complain. Put a band around your wrist during the day, and every time you complain or think about complaining, snap the elastic. This will make you aware of when you complain. You will correlate complaining and pain. Instead, then say three good things that are empowering – or for which you are grateful. Do something pleasant to set this new track in your brain like rub your hands together gleefully.

3. Create a complaint-free zone – For example, your kitchen table or your office space. Never let anything but good thoughts into your chosen space.

4. Worriers – An assignment for you is to take a piece of paper and write down all the things you worry about. Then another piece of paper for all the worries that have come to pass. We are sure you will be surprised to find it is a very short list. The take-away is: Stop worrying.

Attitude forms personal development, and you shared earlier that nothing affects more aspects of your life than attitude. It changes your emotional state, your personality, your social interactions, your health, and your career. Being aware of the negative impacts of attitude will generate antibodies to remove the attitude-disease epidemic.

Dr. Lycka: I also agree with what you said earlier, referencing Earl Nightingale's definitive text on attitude. Your attitude clearly determines what happens to you in life. Your attitude determines whether or not you will enjoy it and finish it successfully. And two people in my life taught me a lot about attitude: Bruce Kirkland, head of Lexus of Edmonton and Dr. David Martz. Bruce taught me that everyone deserves respect and David taught me how important it is to live.

Harriet: You agree with me, again?

Dr. Lycka: Yikes! I said that out loud. You are now sworn to secrecy, Harriet.

GOLDEN PEARL #9

THANKFULNESS

Being thankful for this breath in and out of my lungs, knowing that this will one day cease, is what keeps my heart beating for the next smile, the next sunrise, and the sound of the next little girl's giggle." - Dr. Allen Lycka

Santa Story

I was in my office when a sad-looking 50ish woman by the name of Mary came in. It was the beginning of December and she had been referred for a lesion suspicious of being skin cancer. I took one look and I was convinced it was.

This lady was disheveled. She looked like she hadn't bathed in weeks. I asked her where she lived.

"On the streets," she said.

"Do you have any family?" I asked.

"No."

I knew I was in for a challenge. I phoned the family doctor who had referred her. They told me that she once was a concert pianist, who had a mental breakdown and became schizophrenic. She ended up on the streets.

I insisted social services become involved. I knew Mary needed an operation and soon. She also needed a safe place for the wound to heal. We got her into a living facility, a fancy name for a flophouse. In pre-op, I asked her, "What is Santa bringing you for Christmas?"

"Santa never comes to my house," she retorted.

This haunted me. My staff knew a project had begun in my mind. In our meeting, they agreed Santa must make an appearance for Mary.

We knew the address, but still didn't expect the building to be so decrepit. People passed out in the hallway, likely just steps from where others were shooting drugs in their hardened veins in dark corners.

We hid our discomfort in these unfamiliar surroundings while we bribed the desk clerk, then delivered the basket to her room. Two of my staff took turns hefting that weighty basket up the stairs. We had stuffed it with crackers, jam, dark Belgian chocolate, olives, Italian dried and aged salami, cheese nibbles individually wrapped, hot chocolate powders and speciality coffee that could be made with hot water and oh so much more. One staff member carried a life-size pink fluffy teddy bear that carried the aroma of sun-dried laundry.

After Christmas, a transformed Mary arrived for her follow-up appointment. Edmonton, in a shockingly warm reprieve from old man winter, must have inspired her to shower and don a dress. Her appearance so vibrant, we didn't need to ask how her Christmas was. Curiosity couldn't hold us back.

She was beaming. "Santa found me this Christmas. I can't remember when I last felt like I had a guardian angel. Pink was my favourite colour as a child. How did Santa know? I hung on to that teddy bear. Burying my face in that soft pink fuzzy bear's neck was the first time I breathed without fear. It was the most beautiful Christmas, ever. I'm still enjoying the hot chocolate when I want to feel special."

Sadly, after one more appointment, we lost track. Even more so than many of my patients, she was completely absent from my world. Yet she still serves me as a reminder for what I do have. She came into my life and I am grateful for the lessons she taught me. Able to help her in this brief encounter, I hold this memory as a teacher and companion in my own journey.

"Living in a state of gratitude is the gateway to grace."
- Arianna Huffington. Shared on Twitter in 2014.

Harriet: The definition of thankful is someone feeling or showing gratitude. When you are pleased and are grateful for what you have, it makes you happy and humble. I will use an example from my childhood.

I was going through an advanced case of stinking thinking at age 11. I remember complaining to my father that I was the only one in the world who didn't have the latest trendy shoes. I decided that I was going to prove my point by not eating. My parents let me go through my stinking thinking. I knew eventually they would break down and buy me the shoes because no parent wants their child to starve.

At the time, we lived in Nairobi, Kenya. My father asked me to go to the market with him. He was going to buy my mother imported small bananas from Uganda that the local vendors sold. We saw a mother carrying a child on her back who looked like she was around three years old. The child was crying hysterically. She looked hungry. The mother could not give the child the bananas as it was part of the income she needed to support her family. My father bought six bananas and gave the mother three of them to share with her child. The mother was in tears and was so thankful. She immediately gave the child a banana. The child stopped crying.

There I was ungrateful for the abundance I had. This mother was grateful for what my father did. My father told me that there are no ordinary moments. This experience was to teach me a lesson. We must never take things for granted. Now I live with an attitude of gratitude. And any occurrences of stinking thinking is few and far in between now.

Dr. Lycka: Giving thanks for things and realizing that there is something to be happy about changes your perception of life. It turns from having a 'me' focus to a focus on others. Let me tell you a story.

A poor man came to my office itching like crazy. I looked at him, carefully examined him and found scabies, a mite that lived under his skin. I told him he must treat himself with a medication on two separate occasions and wash all his clothing and bedding. He looked at me. "How sir, I have no money and I live on the street?"

To apply the medication, he had to shower first and apply after showering. He had no access to a shower or another set of clean clothes, so I took him to the local clothing store and bought him three new outfits, then to the pharmacy for his medication and then to the Royal Glenora Club and had him shower and helped him apply the medication after he showered on two occasions. I gave him all the change I had on me to go to the laundromat so he could wash all his possessions.

I saw him one month later for follow-up and his itching had stopped. He looked and acted like a new man.

Harriet: That is an amazing story. Any bad thought I had of you is now eliminated.

Dr. Lycka: Harriet, you surprised me. You have negative thoughts about me?

Harriet: Only on my off days. Truth be told, I couldn't agree more. What you focus on is what you are going to see. If you focus on negative things, you will see negative things. When I work with young girls on self-esteem, one of their challenges is often self-love.

The example I share with the students is the one I got from Tony Robbins' 'Power of Focus' session that I attended years back when I was working on my high-performance journey. He used the example of racing cars. When the vehicle starts to skid, instinct is to look at the wall where you are going to avoid the accident. Professional auto racers unconsciously steer in the direction of the open track because they know the outcome if they focus on the wall. What you focus on is what you will get. If you focus on the idea of failing, you will fail because your mind is revealing or manifesting ways to fail.

Dr. Lycka: What guidance do you offer them?

Harriet: I let them know that the first step to loving yourself is shifting your focus. It's hard to come from the point of hating yourself to loving yourself. Recalling happy times leads us to feelings of gratitude.

I remember having lunch with a few teen girls. One stood up and talked about how she hated her legs. Another stood up and said, "My legs are too pale." Another, "Mine are too skinny." Another, " Mine are too muscular." Another, "Mine have too many scars." It was interesting to listen to them competing about who could hate their legs the most. It also confirmed to me what I read about how every woman on the planet struggles with loving every part of their body.

Dr. Lycka: Every man too.

Harriet: I decided to change their focus.

I stood up and asked them if they might allow me to reframe this for them. At their slight nods, I continued. Imagining Amber in my mind, my voice grew quiet, "Girls, imagine if you didn't have any legs?" The image of Amber in her wheelchair came to my mind choking my voice on the last word of the question. My voice held only compassion. Suddenly, they were all quiet. Some lowered their heads or shook their hair in front of their eyes hiding tears. The air was so thick with emotion, I could feel the shift in their attitudes begin. Emotion is as transferable as gratitude and I knew this moment held power. I continued, telling them of Amber who was one of the rare ones not even wishing for the impossible but accepting the impossible that fate had thrown her. Then, of the people out there in the world who would give anything to have legs. They wouldn't care if they were fat, skinny, or scarred.

Taking a moment to be grateful for what you have when thinking of those who have not... puts things in perspective.

> *"I cried because I had no shoes until I met a man who had no feet."– Author unknown*

Dr. Lycka: The Power of Gratitude is contagious. Actor Matthew McConaughey stated during his Oscar speech that it was a scientific fact that gratitude reciprocates. It time travels never knowing who it's going to touch or how many lives it will change.

I once had the pleasure of helping a lady, now called a sex trade worker, badly tattooed by her pimp. The tattoos padlocked her to the street life. She was referred to me by one of the social workers who walked the streets at night to offer support. They called asking me to see this woman. I asked Destiny what she wanted.

She said, "I want out of this life, to have a child, a regular job and to be out forever."

"Tattoo removal is very expensive."

"I don't control my money. I can't pay your fee."

"My charge is not dollars."

She looked at me, confused.

"This is my fee: Number 1, you leave the trade. Number 2, you must pay it forward. That will be the hardest for you to make the internal changes. Number 3, you must show up for every appointment. You have to make every appointment or be banished to never return."

Four years later she returned after her tattoo removal treatment. Peeking over her shoulder in a sling, a curly haired baby smiled, then hid her face. "I just wanted you to know, I'm a social worker now. My husband works by day and I am out at night paying it forward."

Harriet: When I was growing up, my father told me this short story of Mahatma Gandhi that has stayed with me:

"As Gandhi stepped aboard a train one day, one of his shoes slipped off and landed on the track. He was unable to retrieve it as the train started rolling. To the amazement of his companions, Gandhi calmly took off his other shoe and threw it back along the track to land close to the first shoe. Asked by a fellow passenger why he did that, Gandhi replied, "The poor man who finds the shoe lying on the track will now have a pair he can use."

Dr. Lycka: I'm not sure when. I just know it has become a necessity in my life. Even in the hustle and bustle of a busy restaurant, I can press pause, enter my own zone of silence and picture all I am grateful for and this is my secret weapon to the daily stresses of the 21st century. Those of us who have mastered this art, owe it to teach others. We all need to press pause, reflect, and be grateful, even if all we can identify in one given moment is the sunrise, another day, a moment to reflect at a red light. Someone will always let you know if you've meditated too long when the light turns green.

Harriet: Mmm...not always. Here's why I say what I am saying. Since day one, all my children: Tristan, Rhiannah, and Aaliyah, never slept. One Saturday evening, I took my youngest daughter, Aaliyah, who was just five months old, to the ER (Emergency Room). Her temperature soaring, her skin so hot to my touch, I flinched. I complained to the lady sitting next to me in the waiting room. "I'm so sleep deprived. I wish Aaliyah would give me a break."

She might have thought she was being helpful telling me of her best friend, who had lost her baby at birth. Sillborn. "You should be grateful for your baby."

The guilt brought up by the comparison did not fill me with gratitude. I felt horrible. Gratitude can be difficult, especially when our reality is discounted. My pain and stress was real for me. Science tells us of all the hormone shifts we go through after giving birth and then the actual effects on the body of sleep deprivation also left me in no shape to access gratitude. I was at my lowest low. I've had to teach myself to really dig for it in moments like that. It is not always easy. I feel like I missed the gene for gratitude and have had to cultivate it in a disciplined way.

Dr. Lycka: No doubt that moment was awkward for you at the ER, but I would guess gratitude grew in the future for you in the moments looking at all your children despite the sleep deprivation. Like everything, gratitude is something we all must work on individually and cannot be forced on anyone. Gratitude is like an orchid for some and a patch of weeds for others.

Harriet: I may have to take classes on how to care for orchids! I did decide I needed a practice to start the day with specific gratitude as a way to remind myself how blessed I am. Some mornings it goes like this: "I am grateful to have a friend like you, Dr. Lycka, to support me in my journey."

Dr. Lycka: You are just buttering me up again for something. What is it this time?

Harriet: Accept the compliment and hush. I am serious.

Don't give me that look. Listen. Starting with even the smallest thing makes keeping a gratitude journal easier. I am shocked at how a day fills with bumps and obstacles if I skip starting it with my five minutes of gratitude writing. Red lights seem longer, service people sound sharper, more phone calls with irritating interruptions. On the days I insist with my rushing self to slow down and do my gratitudes, it sets everything in flow. I only recognize it in hindsight. The attitude of gratitude changes my mindset. That's the only explanation.

Dr. Lycka: The simple act of gratitude is anything but simple: it has far-reaching implications. The science proves it.

Here's a Gratitude Wheel that shows how gratitude transforms one's life. This can be personalized to fulfill one's journey.

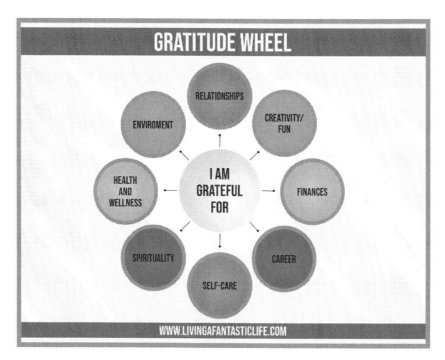

Harriet: Wow. It's like a selfie of your life. It creates a visual of where you are presently and where you want to go. It is so impactful. An act of gratitude affects most major spheres of your life: emotional, personal, social, even your health and career.

> *"I've been really trying to practice the Oprah Winfrey ritual: I check in with gratitude and grace when I wake up. I can be in a little bit of a state of overwhelm and panic if I don't start out being connected to grace and gratitude."*
> *- Kerry Washington said in her May 2017,*
> *Glamour magazine cover story*

Dr. Lycka: Let's take a look at the 'science' of gratitude.

Science has shown that writing in a gratitude journal even five minutes a day can increase your long-term overall happiness by more than 10 percent. That's the same impact as doubling your income! But the benefits are even more immense.

Harriet: There is a simple reason why a five-minute a day gratitude journal can make us so much happier. The real amount of gratitude produced during those five minutes is small, but the emotions of gratitude felt during those five-minutes changing our attitude, triggering a grateful mood, activating a cascade of events – a virtual windfall. When we feel gratitude, it will be more intense and held for longer, and we will feel gratitude for more things at the same time.

In six words, – Gratitude is a positive feedback cycle.

Dr. Lycka: When people are repeatedly exposed to the same emotion, especially if it's intense, they tend to experience less of the feeling. They get numb to it. They attenuate to it.

Simply put, we get used to the good things that happen to us, which also means that we get numb to the bad things that happen to us as well.

But even those who have been disabled have a remarkable ability to rebound. Initially, they may feel terrible, but after months or years, they are on average just as happy as everyone else. I think they are often happier because their disability has opened their eyes to a new life of caring and gratitude.

Numbing to things in our environment is called 'Hedonic adaptation', and it allows us to function in our fast-paced world where something is thrown at us every 30 seconds. It also kills our marriages; we get used to our amazing spouse (or kids, or job, or house, or car, or game). It destroys our drive.

To prevent this, gratitude is one of the most powerful tools in our arsenal.

> *"I try to start every day and end every day by taking a moment to be grateful." – Olivia Wilde, the Booksmart director told Time.*

Harriet: I bet there are thousands of things that gratitude does.

Dr. Lycka: You are so right. And we can write a whole book on them, and maybe we will. But let's go on to explain how anyone can use gratitude in their daily life.

> *"When I started counting my blessings, my whole life turned around."– Willie Nelson, the singer and songwriter wrote in* The Tao of Willie: A Guide to the Happiness in Your Heart.

Harriet: My morning ritual is to wake up at 5 and avoid my phone for an hour. Instead, I focus on my morning seeds, my morning gratitude list.

I start with specific gratitude, "Today I Am Thankful For my family for giving me the freedom to pursue my dreams." I write down at least three things. This reminds me just how much I do have to be thankful for.

There are things that we all take for granted – maybe the roof over our head, the love of our spouse or our parents, the warm clothes on our backs. But for many people in the world, they do not have basic necessities. Food, water, and shelter, along with many other things.

Dr. Lycka: But my list starts even more fundamental than that. I'm grateful for the fact that I can breathe, for the heart beating blood in my chest, for waking up every day and getting out of bed, for the fact that I am even alive, I am grateful. Being an asthmatic makes breath even more precious. We forget about those things from time to time. Until of course these things come into jeopardy.

Harriet: Gratitude can change your life because it makes you thankful for what you have rather than what you want. Gratitude is the single most potent source of inspiration that any person can tap into and it's so simple to apply. All you need to do is just stop and pay attention to the pure beauty and miracle of life around you. It's there for you to see.

"Gratitude is the closest thing to beauty manifested in an emotion."– Mindy Kaling wrote in her 2015 New York Times bestseller Why Not Me?

GOLDEN PEARL #10

TENACITY

I'm tenacious. I think - I know - and I do also have a quality where if you tell me I can't do something, if I know I can't do it, I'm the first to raise my hand and say, "I can't do that." But there is a big Bronx New York Jew in me that says, "Really? You think "Yes I can…Yes I can do it. I Can Do It !!!! - Ellen Barkin

The Man Who Was A Failure

Probably the greatest example of persistence is Abraham Lincoln. If you want to learn about somebody who didn't quit, look no further.

Born into poverty, Lincoln was faced with defeat throughout his life. He lost eight elections, twice failed in business, and suffered a nervous breakdown.

He could have quit many times – but he didn't, and because he didn't quit, he became one of the greatest Presidents in the history of the United States.

Lincoln was a champion, and he never gave up. Here is a sketch of

Lincoln's road to the White House:

1816: His family was forced out of their home. He had to work to support them.

1818: His mother died.

1831: Failed in business.

1832: Ran for state legislature – lost.

1832: Also lost his job – wanted to go to law school but couldn't get in.

1833: Borrowed some money from a friend to begin a business, and by the end of the year, he was bankrupt. He spent the next 17 years of his life paying off this debt.

1834: Ran for state legislature again – won.

1835: Was engaged to be married, sweetheart died and his heart was broken.

1836: Had a total nervous breakdown and was in bed for six months.

1838: Sought to become speaker of the state legislature – defeated.

1840: Sought to become elector – defeated.

1843: Ran for Congress – lost.

1846: Ran for Congress again – this time he won – went to Washington and did a good job.

1848: Ran for re-election to Congress – lost.

1849 Sought the job of land officer in his home state – rejected.

1854: Ran for Senate of the United States – lost.

1856: Sought the Vice-Presidential nomination at his party's national convention – got less than 100 votes.

1858: Ran for U.S. Senate – again, he lost.

1860: Elected president of the United States.

- Author Unknown

Moral of the Story – Tenacity determines one's destiny

*"What is tenacity? The act of being persistent.
Now, what is persistence? Persistence is tenacity."
– Dr. Allen Lycka*

Harriet: I like your quote but would rephrase it. Tenacity and persistence are sisters. Tenacity is persistence with an attitude.

Dr. Lycka: I like that. Let me ask a question. Irrepressible spirit meets immovable force. Which wins?

Harriet: I would bet on the irrepressible spirit. Tenacity carries the day.

Dr. Lycka: I agree. If there is one attribute that determines success, it's tenacity. It's not intelligence. There are lots of underachieving smart people. And lazy rich people. Some wealthy people get there because of family inheritance, luck, or just randomness. And it's not skill. But those who bring tenacity and perseverance always succeed.

*"If you are determined enough and willing to pay the price,
you can get it done." – Mike Ditka, Coach of the Chicago
Bears, a Superbowl Winner*

Harriet: We said this before, but it's worth repeating. Tenacity is persistence with an attitude.

Dr. Lycka: I have a story of pure tenacity. You heard it before, but this time I'm going to elaborate more.

A little girl, aged three, decided it was time to tie her shoelaces.

"Dad, show me how." I did.

She tried over and over to tie those laces and failed each time. We tried another way. Again, she tried again and again, failing each time.

We went to Toys "R" Us and found a clown doll with shoelaces to tie. Mr. Clown became her best friend. He went everywhere she went. She ate with Mr. Clown. She slept with this crazy doll. She played non-stop with Mr. Clown's shoelaces.

And the object, always the object of her game was to tie the laces. After hundreds of attempts, the moment she succeeded, she dropped Mr. Clown. The frown of frustration and concentration switched to a smile wider than I had ever seen. Almost four years old, she attacked me in a gleeful hug I can still feel in my bones. She tied those laces. She kept at this task to master the skill with a perseverance to match any top athlete. Everybody can learn from this kind of tenacity.

Years later, she decided to be a Home Stager. This was before home staging was popular. She found a mentor and learned the skill. She even wrote a book about it by the age of 18.

This girl exemplifies tenacity. She's my youngest daughter, Stephanie.

Harriet: She is unstoppable. Let's explore the ways any person can learn from Stephanie.

Dr. Lycka: One way is to choose role models. What does that mean? I guess if you have role models who are tenacious, you can pattern yourself after them.

Harriet: Another way is to fix your belief system. The number one reason people give up is that they carry false beliefs in their minds, such as:

1. I don't have the right genetics or

2. I am not lucky

"People of mediocre ability sometimes achieve outstanding success because they don't know when to quit. Most men succeed because they are determined to." – George Allan

Dr. Lycka: Poppycock. It's not what you are born with. It's what you do with that. Malcolm Gladwell discussed this in his best-seller, *Outliers*. He said that to become an expert, it takes 10,000 hours (or approximately ten years) of deliberate practice. But deliberate practice is a specifically defined term. It involves goal setting, quick feedback, and countless drills to improve skills with an eye on mastery. Integral to this is to have a written plan and goals. Goals are dreams with a deadline.

And David Martz showed me how important it is to do it now. Without his help in Colorado Spings, I might not be writing these words now.

Harriet: Another is to heed your own advice. Don't listen to the negative criticism of others.

Dr. Lycka: I know that all too well. When I decided to be a Dermatologist, many, many people tried to dissuade me. I was undaunted. I applied to hundreds of schools, only to be rejected.

My mother-in-law asked, "When are you going to give up your foolish dream?"

Unperturbed, I tried again. And I got accepted.

I then decided to do Cosmetic Dermatology. There were no training schools, so I went on to train myself. And many feel I became very good at it.

Harriet: I will vouch for that. You were the best, and I have seen it first-hand.

Dr. Lycka: Thanks for the compliment. Let's say I was okay. I knew one or two things about one or two things.

Harriet: That's my favorite quote from you. You are so humble.

Another thing you can do is to remove emotions from the equation if you are looking to be successful. Keep moving even when you don't feel like it. One of the most common reasons that people give up is believing that they should only do things when they feel like it.

Hard work, even when you feel you can't do it, often results in success over failure. That's tenacity.

Dr. Lycka: When I wanted to get into med school, it was very competitive. I worked harder than the average students. Most university students would take Friday nights off and party. I worked. Did I feel like it? Hell, no. But I did it anyway.

Harriet: I can say the same for my death races. Once, I had a stress fracture on my right leg and had to have an air cast boot. It would have been a good excuse not to train. I still went to the gym, but took precautions not to re-injure myself. I admit, some-days, I didn't feel like it. But I trained anyway.

Dr. Lycka: Here's another crucial fact: there are no genes for will and tenacity! I bet that surprises you, right?

Harriet: A bit, but it's probably true.

Dr. Lycka: Here's a clue. You need to refuel often. Take a break, then get back to it. But don't break for too long.

In writing this chapter, I went to bed at 10 PM. I got up at 3 AM. My writing muse was awake, so I wrote. I suppose I should call her 'tenacity' because she always pushes me.

Harriet: I admire that in you. You put yourself under pressure by eliminating the option of giving up. That means you either make it or lose everything.

Dr. Lycka: It's empowering to be surrounded by tenacious peo-ple. It becomes contagious and keeps you driven.

Harriet: Here's my personal favourite: Using the Power of Re-venge.

Dr. Lycka: What does that mean?

Harriet: It's not the 'eye for an eye strategy'. It is a restoration for self-esteem and trajectory to other people's negative words to restore balance and dignity. For instance, tell people about your plans, they will laugh at you, you will get charged, and you will find it much harder to give up. As a result, you will have the last laugh. It's the point of no return when you share your BHAG

(Big Hairy Audacious Goal) where you have to then prove yourself or give them the right to continue laughing. I am too stubborn to allow that.

Dr. Lycka: Remind me to not ever stand in your way. I'm sure I would be ploughed down. Thankfully, we all have what it takes to be tenacious. You can always build up your resolve by using some of the tips mentioned above, but don't forget that it's been there all along. Everything you need, you already have. Just have to recognize it and work at it.

"Many of life's failures are people who did not realize how close they were to success when they gave up."
– Thomas A. Edison

"You are the only problem you have ever had and you are the only solution you will ever have." – Bob Proctor

Harriet: Here's my story on persistence.

A teenage daughter asks her Dad, 'Can I have the keys to the car? I want to go out tonight with some friends.'

Dad: Did you clean your room?

Teenage Daughter: No.

Dad: Did you do your homework?

Teenage Daughter: No.

Dad: Did you help clean up your dishes after supper?

Teenage Daughter: No.

Dad: Then, the answer is **NO**.

Teenage Daughter: Mom, can I have the keys to the car? I want to go out tonight with some friends?

Mom: What did your dad say?

Teenage Daughter: He said no, but...

Mom: No buts. Why are you asking me?

Teenage Daughter: I'm trying to practice how to be tenacious."

Dr. Lycka: Yup, that's tenacity.

Harriet: No, that's manipulation.

GOLDEN PEARL #11

LAUGHTER

"An onion can make people cry but there's never been a vegetable that can make people laugh." – Will Rogers

The Camel

I was in Egypt at the Pyramids of Giza, and I decided to get a picture on a camel. Do you know what a camel is?

A camel is a jackass crossed with a giraffe. They are on stilts. No, giant. No, giant stilts. And they smell and spit. They are pig-headed varmints with arsenic personalities.

My tour guide arranged for me to meet the owner of the camels and told me he would get his gentlest camel.

By his guilty-looking face, I knew something was afoot.

This camel was lying down, enjoying a mid-afternoon snooze and he wasn't going to do anything.

The camel driver said, "Get on."

I sheepishly obeyed.

Then he turned to the camel and said, "Get up" in Arabic.

No go. For the next 10 minutes, he cajoled, begged, threatened and beat the camel to get up.

The camel got up – on his front knees.

But he was mad. He showed it: He tried to throw me off the back. I hung on for dear life.

"Get up," the camel driver yelled at the camel again.

He refused. Then the same cajoling, begging, threatening, and beating ritual ensued.

He got up, begrudgingly. But he was madder. He spit. He growled that guttural growl only camels can make.

But just on his back knees. And he tried to throw me off the front, but with even more force.

I looked around and saw boulders the size of Volkswagens around me.

I knew if I was thrown off, I was going to be seriously injured, maybe even die. I hung on for dear life.

"Get up," demanded the camel driver to the camel, and the same process repeated until the camel got all the way up.

But this time he was really angry. He tried to throw me off again and again and again. I thought I was on a bucking bronco at the Calgary Stampede.

Hurriedly, I begged my wife to get a picture of me on that camel. She did.

"Get me down," I demanded.

"Are you sure, sir?" asked the camel driver.

"Yes, immediately." I insisted as I started to turn green.

So, then he started the same process I went through to get up, in reverse – first front knees, then back knees, etc.

You know the story. And at each step, the camel tried to throw me off. I was like a mouse trying to ride a rabid elephant. First, when he got on his front knees, then his back.

And finally, when I got off, I kissed the ground.

"Praise to Allah," I shouted.

The camel driver said, "Just kidding, he's not my gentlest camel. At least not today, anyway," he said. "Don't know what happened. Let me buy you a coke.

"No, I'm ok."

"I will be insulted if you don't let me buy you a coke."

So, I had a coke with a camel driver from Egypt to end a near-death experience with a camel.

Yes, things go better with Coca-Cola™. I am sure glad camels can't fly.

- Dr. Allen Lycka

Moral of the Story – Laughter needs to be in your everyday life.

Dr. Lycka: I want to touch on one of the most important pearls. It's laughter.

Mark Twain said, *"[Humanity] has unquestionably one weapon— laughter. Power, money, persuasion, supplication, persecution—these can lift at a colossal humbug—push it a little—weaken it a little, century by century, but only laughter can blow it to rags and atoms at a blast. Against the assault of laughter, nothing can stand."*

Harriet: That's profound. I do think we take ourselves too seriously.

Dr. Lycka: Yes, and related to this, William Thackeray wrote: *"A good laugh is sunshine in the house."*

Harriet: One of the reasons I like to get together with you is that you always make me laugh. Everything you said is correct. I love you for making me laugh even when I don't want to.

Madeleine L 'Engle, an American writer, said, "A good laugh heals a lot of hurts."

Dr. Lycka: Yes, it does. I think laughter is proof there is a benevolent higher being who cares for mankind.

Laughter, especially at oneself, tempers ego, interrupts narcissism and improves your happiness in the moment. It keeps you positively moving forward.

Harriet: Let's explore ways to do this. One way is to seek out people that love to laugh and avoid those who tend to be dour and depressed.

Dr. Lycka: It's true if you want happiness – hang with happy people.

"You can't deny laughter; when it comes, it plops down in your favorite chair and stays as long as it wants."
– Stephen King

Harriet: Another way to learn how to laugh is to learn how to play.

Dr. Lycka: That is entirely true. I find I laugh a lot when I play with my grandchildren. Laughter also occurs when I play games.

"I always knew looking back on my tears would bring me laughter, but I never knew looking back on my laughter would make me cry." – Cat Stevens

Harriet: Another way is to play with pets.

Dr. Lycka: I'm a huge dog lover. They always make me laugh. One day, my daughter Steph was over at our house with her dog, Jango. He loves playing 'chase me'. There are howls of laughter as he runs around our house, and I try to catch him.

Harriet: Another idea is you can watch funny movies.

Dr. Lycka: Ever hear of *Patch Adams*?

Harriet: I think so. It was a movie by Robin Williams, Right?

Dr. Lycka: The movie called *Patch Adams* starred Robin Williams and was based on a book called *Gesundheit!* written by a doctor who dresses as a clown and told the architect designing his new health center in West Virginia to 'make it goofy', with trap doors, eyeball-shaped exam rooms, and chandeliers to swing on. Here's a quote by him:

"Laughter releases endorphins and other natural mood elevating and pain-killing chemicals, improves the transfer of oxygen and nutrients to internal organs. Laughter boosts the immune system and helps the body fight off disease, cancer cells as well as viral, bacterial and other infections. Being happy is the best cure of all diseases!"

Harriet: Let's end this chapter with a laugh.

Dr. Lycka: Ok, here's a joke:

A boy goes to his mother and says, "I don't want to go to school today."

The mother asks: "Are you sick?"

The boy says, "No."

"Why, do you want to stay home?"

The boy says, "The kids don't like me. The teachers shun me. Everyone hates me. I don't want to go."

The mother says, "You have to go. You're not sick. And you are 46 years old and the principal."

Harriet: I have an even funnier story.

I had just arrived in Paris for my first photo-shoot as a young model – dressed to the nines as this was a top agency, and I had landed a great gig. I was in the waiting room of the modelling agency waiting to see my agent. Across the room, I noticed a stunning woman who looked up, smiled and said hi to me. She was friendly, curious and even complimented my looks. I wasn't in the mood for small talk, so I simply rolled my eyes and made it clear she was getting into my space. In an attempt to brush her off completely, I started bragging in an almost condescending way, on how I was going to be on page three of Vogue magazine – and needed to focus. I told her

I preferred to be left alone. Then when my agent came out to greet me, she gestured to the friendly woman across from me and asked, "Have you met our top model – who by the way, will be on the cover of the same magazine?"

The embarrassment of that moment knocked me down more than a couple of notches. Some much-needed humility was injected into my being that day. Over the years, my embarrassment gave way to laughter. I now look back on that self-aggrandizing, younger version of myself and chuckle.

GOLDEN PEARL #12

ENTHUSIASM

It is not success that brings enthusiasm. It is the enthusiasm that brings success. – Ralph Waldo Emerson

Fred the Carpenter

It was a cold November day. Fred was tired. He had worked 35 years for his boss but could not rustle up any more enthusiasm to do so. So he went to his boss and said, "It's time for me to quit."

His boss thought about it for a moment. He said, "Before you quit, can you do one more job for me? I need a special house built, and you are the only one I'd trust to do it."

Begrudgingly, Fred said yes. But he had no enthusiasm. He got to work late and left early. His work was barely passable. It was so bad that when the house was done, it barely passed inspection.

When he was finished, Fred delivered the keys on his boss' desk. Fred said, "Ok, I'm done."

The boss said, "Not so fast."

He called all the employees together.

"Everyone, this is Fred's last day. He has been my loyal employee for 30 years. Now I have a special surprise for Fred. For the last year, Fred has been involved in a very special project. He has built me one last house. Now, today, I am giving this house to Fred. I hope you enjoy this in your retirement.

- *Author unknown*

Moral of the story: Bring your enthusiasm every day.

"Enthusiasm glows, radiates, permeates and immediately captures everyone's interest." – Paul Meyer

Dr. Lycka: Let's chat about Golden Pearl #12. ENTHUSIASM. It's one of my favourites.

Harriet: I agree.

Dr. Lycka: Wow, it's a rare day.

Harriet: We actually agree on a lot of things. Enthusiasm is the spark you bring to daily life that starts the fire.

Dr. Lycka: I think Woody Allen said: *"To succeed in life, you have to show up."*

Harriet: No, he said, *"80% of success is showing up."*

Dr. Lycka: O.K. smarty. What's the other 20%?

Harriet: I think the other 20% is enthusiasm.

Dr. Lycka: And then the other 1% must be?

Harriet: ???I'm an accountant. That makes no sense.

Dr. Lycka: I've never seen an enthusiastic person stop at 100%. That's a start.

Harriet: Now, I see your point.

Dr. Lycka: And as a doctor, what is the most contagious thing in the world?

Harriet: As I write this? COVID-19 - the nouveau corona virus.

It's sweeping the planet. But it, too, shall pass. But, of course, it's enthusiasm, the topic of this chapter.

Dr. Lycka: Bingo. It's also incurable, COVID-19 hopefully will soon be tamed.

> *"I play to win, whether during practice or a real game. And I will not let anything get in the way of me and my competitive enthusiasm to win." – Michael Jordan*

Harriet: Enthusiasm: An infectious, incurable disease.

Dr. Lycka: Yup. One which hopefully starts in childhood. Let's look at this through the eyes of a three-year-old. Take, for example, my grandson Zach. It was frightfully cold in Edmonton, -40 below Celsius.

Yet Zach went outside and said, "Grandpa, look," as he looked into the air. "Look at what, Zach?" I asked, and he responded, "The diamonds in the air."

It was so cold; ice crystals had formed. The sunlight was making them glisten.

To Zach, they looked like diamonds in the sky.

Harriet: That's enthusiasm. Let me tell you a story:

Two frogs fell into a can of cream,

Or so it has been told:

The sides of the can were shiny and steep,

The cream was deep and cold.

"Oh, what's the use?" said number one,

"It's plain to see; no help's around.

Good-bye, my friend, good-bye, sad world"

And weeping still, he drowned.

But number two, of sterner stuff,

Dog-paddled in surprise.

Then while he licked his creamy lips

And blinked his creamy eyes

"I'll swim at least awhile," he thought.

Or so it has been said.

"It really wouldn't help the world

If one more frog were dead."

An hour or more he kicked and swam,

Not once he stopped to mutter;

Then hopped out from the island that he made

of fresh churned butter.

- *Author Unknown*

Dr. Lycka: So now you are telling me enthusiasm is not only infectious. It makes butter?!

Harriet: Just like you to focus on food when we are talking about enthusiasm. Focus.

Dr. Lycka: Food is always important. But we will come back to food in Book 2.

> *"Enthusiasm is a volcano on whose top never grows the grass of hesitation." – Kahlil Gibran*

Harriet: Do you know how to keep enthusiasm in your life?

Dr. Lycka: I think so. As you know, many call me Dr. Enthusiasm.

Harriet: How did you get that way?

Dr. Lycka: I guess I could say that it's as simple as being enthusiastic. My friend, Paula Abdul, said, "Fake it until you make it." I don't think many know, but Paula is amazing. She was born with one leg inches shorter than the other. When she'd cry as a baby, her lungs would collapse. She learned never to cry. But this did not dissipate her enthusiasm. She learned to be a world-class dancer and then started the dance craze in cheerleading, when she was on the LA Lakers cheerleading team.

Harriet: I would add another thing to this. I'd say you should spend at least 15 minutes a day on something you love.

Dr. Lycka: That's easy for me. I have dozens of passions.

Harriet: I like physical activities, all that body movement, especially death races, you know. It's a powerful mood buster – more effective than drugs or shopping therapy.

Dr. Lycka: Here's another. Practice self-compassion.

Self-compassion is the practice of noticing what you're feeling, remembering that you're human (and therefore fallible, just like everyone else on the planet), and treating yourself with the same kindness you'd give to a beloved friend. Unfortunately, few of us have been trained to respond to ourselves in this way. Much more often, our response is to beat ourselves up when we stumble, but research has shown (and your own experience may echo) that self-flagellation is counterproductive.

Harriet: I like to spend time with enthusiastic people – like you. Enthusiasm is contagious. Since your time and energy are limited, pay attention to how you feel after spending time with people in your life, and seek out those who fill you up, energize and inspire you.

Dr. Lycka: Here's one more: practice spontaneous acts of kindness (but not sacrifice). Have you ever noticed how good it feels to say or do something kind for someone else? Performing random, spontaneous acts of kindness – even just a kind word or a genuine smile – has been shown to boost self-image, lead us to perceive others more compassionately, promote a greater sense of connection with others, and feel grateful for our good fortune. All of these things make us happier, and when we're happier, it's easy to be more enthusiastic.

Don't overdo it at the expense of filling your own bucket.

Harriet: And with that, we need to turn to the last chapter Dr. Lycka.

Dr. Lycka: Yes, it's on Empowerment.

GOLDEN PEARL #13

EMPOWERMENT

"The more you trust your intuition the more empowered you become, the stronger you become, and the happier you become." – Gisele Bundchen

Part 1

Due to the COVID-19 virus, there were a flurry of memes and song parodies bringing a dark brand of humour to the very real situation of the pandemic of 2020.

Uneducated, Naïve Me

I have a cold.

I have arrived from abroad.

I am asked to go into "social isolation."

I listen to Simon and Garfunkel's 'I am a rock'.

I have my books

And my poetry to protect me;

I am shielded in my armor,

Hiding in my room, safe within my womb.

I touch no one and no one touches me.

I am a rock,

I am an island. And a rock feels no pain;

And an island never cries."

Part 2 Me Learning

I walk outside to get a breath of fresh air

I am told by a total stranger that I am not following 'social distancing' requirements

I go to my home again.

I listen to Simon and Garfunkel's 'Sound of Silence'.

Hello darkness, my old friend

I've come to talk with you again

Because a vision softly, creeping

Left its seeds while I was sleeping

And the vision, that was planted in my brain... still remains

Within the sound of silence

Part 3 Educating Me

I walk outside.

I recognize and acknowledge everyone's social distance.

I go home ...it's become a routine...but my eyes have been opened

I listen to Simon and Garfunkel's, 'The Boxer'.

And wishing I was gone

Going home

Where the New York City winters aren't bleeding me

Leading me

Going home

...

Mm-mm-mm

Lie-la-lie

Lie-la-lie-lie-lie-lie-lie

Lie-la-lie

Lie-la-lie-lie-lie-lie-lie, lie-lie-lie-lie-lie

Lie-la-lie-lie-lie-lie-lie Lie-la-lie

Part 4 Learned Me

I learn physical isolation is not social distancing.

I learn there are internet channels that tell me about the world out there. I share my thoughts with people from around the world.

I am not alone.

I listened to Simon and Garfunkel's 'Bridge Over Troubled Water'.

When you're weary, feeling small

When tears are in your eyes, I'll dry them all

I'm on your side, oh, when times get rough

And friends just can't be found

Like a bridge over troubled water

I will lay me down

Part 5 Empowered Me

I love my nest

I again listen to Simon and Garfunkel's "I am a rock"

I've built walls,

A fortress deep and mighty,

That none may penetrate.

I have no need of friendship; friendship causes pain.

But I disagree with the wording and the sentiment.

I am alone, sheltered, but empowered.

- Dr. Allen Lycka

Moral: Empowerment changes your mindset

Harriet: In life we have a choice on which road to walk down. Dr. Lycka, I can't imagine how you must have felt when you heard these words from your doctor "You have Amyotrophic Lateral Sclerosis. (ALS) Lou Gehrig's disease and you have six months to live. Get your affairs in order."

Dr. Lycka: No one wants to hear their life is about to end. I admit it wasn't easy at all. I began to analyze my life. I felt like I had been beaten down, helpless. With patience, time, and support from others, I found a 'different road' to walk on that empowered me. Then I found you to help me on that road.

Harriet: 'Empowered Me' happens to be the name of my Social Enterprise, an organization devoted to inspiring, educating, and supporting girls to develop a sense of purpose by offering workshops, programs, and personal coaching.

Dr. Lycka: How did you start the company?

Harriet: I just found a need in the community and filled it. My life journey thrived when I started teaching extensively in modeling school. I focused on helping the participants develop self-compassion and overcome negative self-talk. My inspiration became so contagious. Soon parents and teens were looking up to me for inspiration. Determined to have a constructive influence on the lives of others, I left the agency and created a mastermind program titled, 'I Believe in Me Because...' to instill this energy in young people.

Dr. Lycka: What an inspiration you are to those young girls!

Harriet: On the contrary, they inspire me to be a better person. I don't know if I ever mentioned to you, but you pushed me to be who I am today.

Dr. Lycka: Little ol' me. How?

Harriet: As a big sponsor for the YWCA Women of Distinction, you opened up a path to inspire young women and girls to make the impossible possible. I was nominated one year, but I didn't win. However, that year I was inspired by what women and girls were doing to build futures – from astronauts, artists, tradeswomen, to politicians – you name it. That was a limitless crowd. I've never had a chance to share this with you. You became my mentor that day when I didn't win. You know how I don't like losing. Thanks for becoming my mentor, my friend, and my inspiration that day. When I grow up, I want to be just like you.

Dr. Lycka: I am speechless.

Harriet: That's possible? You, speechless! While you are sitting there gaping, I will take advantage.

With your inspiration, a student of mine, Anastacio, age 15, told me how I inspired her. It's like a pay-it-forward! Let me share the letter she wrote to me:

Dear Harriet,

Before I started taking the 'Empowered Me' course, I would come home from school, go straight to my room and lock the door. I would throw my books on the bed, go in the bathroom and stare into the mirror. The girl in the mirror would stare me down and tell me that I was hideous, repulsive, stupid, worthless, a failure, and she would say as long as I was still alive, I would never be good enough and would never amount to anything. The girl in the mirror would tell me I was fat, nobody genuinely liked me, and my best effort will never be good enough and that my desires will never be strong enough to achieve my dreams.

I would ask the mirror if what the girl is saying was true. The mirror would always answer back and say, "It's true, my dear, that's how people see you. Remember, I know you best because I see you every day."

I would look in the mirror for a glimpse of hope, but not once did I ever see it. Every day I would hear the voice of the mirror telling me louder and louder that I was not good enough. I would run away from the mirror, not wanting to hear those harsh words. I now see myself as that girl who continues to battle the mirror. But now, the words of the mirror have become weaker. I won't stop fighting until its evil words cease. Thank you for giving me that courage. More importantly, I want to thank you for believing in me and for making a difference in my life. I will always be grateful for the difference you made in my life. I promise to continue working on myself.

> *"I don't like to gamble but if there's one thing I'm willing to bet on, it's myself." – Beyonce*

Harriet: We're at the last chapter, Dr. Lycka, and we've shared lots of ways to live a fantastic life.

Dr. Lycka: Yes, and I think everyone should live every day as if it were their last day on earth.

Harriet: I would hope that those who read this book would live that last day differently.

Dr. Lycka: And if I know you, that day would be an empowered day. Tell me what empowerment really means to you. I mean, Harriet, for the moment I want you to forget about barefoot death race running. It may be hard for you but tell me what empowerment really means for you when your daughter says, 'I want a dog.' Remember you told her it was either you or the dog and she retorted, "Bye Mom, I'm going to miss you."

Harriet: That's not one of my proudest memories. Empowerment, to me, is these three words: 'Believing in Yourself'. It's that 'can-do and will do' mentality and living an intentional life. My formula for empowerment is desire plus confidence plus action. Desire is the first drive toward achievement. Confidence is that uplifting feeling before you understand the situation. Last year I wanted to run the Great Canadian Death Race. I know how you are looking at me Doctor Lycka. Don't interrupt. One of the world's toughest Ultramarathons in less than 24 hours. The desire was there, and I knew I could run it. I trained for more than a year with injuries and used the work-life-balance equation. I leaned on my family, friends, and communities for support. I achieved my goal: there I was standing at the finish line, arms raised, and overcome with emotion. I was beyond thrilled!

Dr. Lycka: Harriet, you're crazy. I've often thought about running marathons. But I let the thoughts pass quickly, sit in my easychair and take a nap. I know you have told me empowerment allows you to live a selfless life. Can you explain that?

Harriet: When I am empowered, I live a selfless life through service. I have always felt a sense of happiness by serving others. Giving my time and lending an ear to another has enriched my life. Three principles guide my beliefs in this arena: I value and serve people, think of ways to add value to people through encouragement and appreciation, and I encourage everyone to see the value in others.

"You will not determine my story, I will." – Amy Schumer

Dr. Lycka: You have been volunteering in palliative care for quite some time now and working with dying people. What are the types of conversations you can share with me?

Harriet: The common theme in their stories is "regret." Margaret was one of the patients who had the biggest impact on my life. The prognosis was bleak; she was given only two months to live. She was in the last chapter of her life. One afternoon, I walked into her room and saw paint tubes strewn about, brushes soaking in murky water, and several beautiful paintings on the floor. Her hands were stained with a mesh of colors. I asked her if the art was hers. Margaret 's eyes welled with tears, and she smiled and asked me to sit beside her. She held my hand and spoke sadly, 'Harriet, I am so afraid. I spend a lot of my time laying here in bed. I have several regrets. I lived a life that others wanted me to live. I never allowed myself to be happy. I was always the peacekeeper and was afraid to tell my loved ones that I cared because I assumed that they knew. I complicated my life with layers upon layers of favours, and chores, and duties all for others. I never paid attention to myself or the fact that I loved to paint. My dream was an afterthought that I kept brushing aside. I kept putting it off because I thought I had more time to live.'

Dr. Lycka: I can see it's impossible for that conversation not to have affected you. How did you feel?

Harriet: It was heartbreaking, but I was honored to have her share her regrets. Margaret was married for 40 years. She never pursued her dreams or lived the life she desired because she wanted to support her husband through law school. They had three beautiful daughters. She participated in all their activities. She was a 'super-mom and super-wife'. She had no time for friends. The children grew up and moved on with their lives. Then, it was time for her to start living. Unfortunately, her husband was diagnosed with dementia. Margaret looked after him for two years until he passed away on their 40th anniversary. Weeks later, she was diagnosed with stage 4 colon cancer. Her life was now that hospital bed in palliative care. She told me soon it would be 'the empty bed' filled with regrets. Margaret said to me, "Live a life that makes you happy and don't die with your canvas half empty."

> *"Whether you think you can, or you think you can't — you're right."– Henry Ford*

Dr: Lycka: That is a strong message from her experiences. What does a day of painting your own canvas look like for you?

Harriet: You're making me recall an experience I had a year ago. A young girl came to me with no hope or love for herself. My solution was to take her for a walk at my favourite park. We took our shoes off and walked on the grass. We heard birds chirping, insects buzzing, and sounds of squirrels rushing from tree to tree along with the rhythmic croaking of frogs. I was at peace hoping this could flow through me to her. We walked in silence for a time. There was dew on the grass, and I could see the brightness of the sun rising. Nothing else mattered to me in the moment. I knew then; I could do what

I desired to do. In that moment, I wanted to do nothing, feel nothing and just be at peace. And I did. I invited her to join me in the magic of the moment, sharing how our minds heed our every command. I also shared with her as we neared the end of our walk, "Whatever you tell your mind, that's the reality that you will live. Take this moment to connect with nature and just be silent. Listen to the flow of water, the squirrels, the frogs and liberate your thoughts. You can repeat this exercise as often as needed.

Dr. Lycka: The Japanese doctors prescribe it to patients. The "drug" is called 'forest bathing.' The power of silencing our minds and being in nature's rhythms is empowering.

***

In sharing our stories and the experiences of others, we hope that our book will enrich and change how you live your life. We have all been through adversities, opened doors for others, have been disappointed from failed plans, and experienced the pain of harsh words. These various experiences converge to tell a story – the story of who you are. No matter what, we each must embrace and own our story. We must take responsibility for our choices and accept where those choices take us. It is important to know who you are, and to commit to living your best life ever. "It is never too late to be who you want to be." So said George Eliot in the 19th century. There is always a new street, a new direction to help you live a fantastic life!

For you to be born in this time and place, the odds were one in 400 trillion. You are a miracle. Start seeing yourself as the marvel that you are and live your life for you.

BONUS GOLDEN PEARL

FEAR

Conquering Fear (An Ethiopian Folktale)

Once upon a time in an Ethiopian village, there lived a young boy who was so fearful of the world around him that his family called him Miobe, frightened one.

"Why do you call me that?" the boy asked his grandfather.

The old man laughed. "Because you are a 'fraidy cat', afraid of your own shadow. If someone said, "Boo" you might hit your head on the ceiling." He chuckled, his big white teeth flashing an affectionate smile. The boy's entire family and neighbours were of the same opinion.

Miobe pondered these words and decided he must find a way to best his fear. So that night when everyone was fast asleep, he packed a sack and set off into the world to find out what it was that scared him so he could vanquish it. He fell asleep under the chilly starry sky, shivering in his blanket. Before drifting off, he loudly said, "I am not afraid. I am NOT afraid." Soon after, he was jarred from his deep sleep by the wolves howling. Disoriented, he originally thought it was a recurring bad dream, where he was chased by wolves and only barely escaped being eaten by them.

But this time, he collected his thoughts as he awakened quickly. Instead of cowering, he walked toward the sound, saying aloud, "I will crush you, fear." He never reached the wolves because they stayed forever in the distance, teasing him to keep approaching.

Soon, a magnificent sun rose to greet the day with warm colors of gold and crimson. He sat on a hill overlooking a great meadow and rejoiced that he had survived the first night. He partook in some dried meat he had in a satchel around his chest and some fresh berries he found on a nearby bush. He quenched his thirst from the stream he shared with the animals gathered there. The day was shaping up to be much better than his night.

"I am becoming brave," he said as he ambled on. Soon he came to a village, and for a moment he thought, "I don't know these people at all. They might be hostile to a stranger." He remembered the talk in his village of head-hunters.

But he straightened up and walked right into the village, saying aloud, "I will conquer you, fear."

He walked into the village square, and there he found the village elders gathered, muttering among themselves. As Miobe came near, they looked up and sneered, "Who are you?"

"I'm traveling the world to become brave," Miobe answered.

The elders laughed. "Fool! No one can find bravery where it does not exist."

"What do you mean?" Miobe asked.

The elders sighed unhappily. "We are finished," said one old man. "Our village is being threatened by a monster up on the mountain."

Miobe followed the old man's gaze to the top of the mountain.

"See him, there," the old man said.

Miobe squinted. He did not want to insult the man, but he saw nothing there.

"Look," said another man. "See? It has the head of a crocodile. A monstrous crocodile!"

"And his body is as horrible as a hippopotamus. A gigantic hippopotamus!"

"It's like a dragon!" another man cried, "with fire shooting from its snout!"

Now Miobe began to see the monster. He began to see the smoke and fire, the wrinkled skin, the fiery eyes. "I see," he said, but silently he promised himself he would not be afraid. So he walked away from the elders, into the village proper.

Everywhere people cringed. The little children hid inside, refusing to go to school. "If the children go outside," the women said, "the monster will come down from the mountain and eat them."

The farmers hovered inside their doorways, hoes and rakes in hand to defend themselves; outside their horses stood ready to take their owners rapidly away. "We cannot work," they told Miobe. "If we go into the fields, the monster will come down and attack us."

Miobe saw wandering goats, sheep and cows out at the edge of the village, but no one came to milk the animals or tend to them. No one planted crops. Few left their homes, preferring to tremble indoors.

"The monster is as big as 10 barges!" they whispered among themselves as Miobe listened. "The monster is going to annihilate us!"

Finally Miobe decided it was up to him to destroy the monster. "I wish to conquer fear," he announced, "and so I shall go slay the monster!"

"No, son, don't do it!" the elders pleaded. Mothers gathered to try to shield the young man from harm. Fathers shook their heads and warned, "You will die."

Miobe shivered and his heart fluttered, but he was determined. "I must conquer fear!" he said, and he set off.

At the base of the mountain, he looked up and felt the chill of fear run down his spine. His legs could barely support him as he forced himself onward. That monster looked even bigger and fiercer than any dragon, more threatening than the pack of wolves that threatened him nightly in his dreams.

He remembered the days when he had been afraid. He had a huge lump in his throat and his whole body was drenched in sweat. He took a deep breath and began to climb.

"I must not fear. Fear is the mind-killer. Fear is the little-death that brings total obliteration. I will face my fear. I will permit it to pass over me and through me. And when it has gone past I will turn the inner eye to see its path. Where the fear has gone there will be nothing. Only I will remain."
— *Frank Herbert, Dune*

As he climbed, he looked up, but now he saw the monster seemed to be growing smaller.

"How peculiar," he said aloud. "My eyes are deceiving me."

He continued to climb.

When he was halfway up, he looked again. He squinted, shielding his eyes, but the monster's eyes no longer seemed so fierce, and the flames no longer shot from its snout.

"The closer I get, the smaller he looks," Miobe said puzzlingly. He continued to climb, though now he pulled his dagger from his sack so that he would be prepared.

As he came around a bend in the path, he saw the summit before him. He gasped. The monster had disappeared.

Miobe turned and looked behind him. Surely the creature was going to sneak up from behind to attack. But when he turned, he saw nothing. He heard nothing. He held his breath. He looked left. He looked right.

He continued to climb.

At long last he reached the summit and all was empty and quiet. Nothing was there.

Suddenly he heard a sound at his feet. He looked down and saw a little creature, just like a toad with wrinkled skin and round, frightened eyes.

He bent down and picked it up. "Who are you?" he asked. "How did you become so small?" But the monster said nothing, and so he cradled it in his hand and walked down the mountain.

When he reached the village, the people cried, "He's safe!" and they surrounded him.

Miobe held out his hand and showed them the tiny wrinkled toad. "This is the monster," he said.

The crowd stood in awe. They looked at the mountain. Where the monster once stood threatening, there was now a beautiful waterfall with a rainbow. They turned to the young hero for an explanation.

"This creature's image was reflected off the rocks and water to appear to look much bigger than he was. But he is just a toad, after all."

"What is your name?" asked the elder. "Miobe" said the young champion.

The creature croaked, and the elder looked up at the crowd and said, "Miobe has brought us the monster. Its name is fear. From this day forward his name will be Jegna Sew New – brave person."

An oral Nigerian Folk Tale as shared by Harriet with Doctor Lycka.

"Bran thought about it. 'Can a man still be brave if he's afraid?' 'That is the only time a man can be brave,' his father told him." — *George R.R. Martin,* A Game of Thrones

Moral of the story: Facing Fear Often Causes Fears to Vanish

Dr. Lycka: The fear response is an adaptive mechanism because it keeps us from injury. That's why it's wired in our primitive brains and initiates a 'fright, flight, fight response' when it occurs. When a wild animal attacks us, we feel fright, we respond by flight or fight.

Harriet: I know fear all too well. When Martin attacked me, I felt true fear and dread. I'm black so it's rare for me to sweat, but that day I was dripping out of every pore. I was paralyzed. When I tried to crawl away, my legs didn't move. My whole body vibrated with that fear. I tried to shout, no sound would leave my throat. My attacker grabbed my neck and strangled me, making me gasp for air. As much as I wanted to get away, my limbs wouldn't listen or respond with the frantic messages my brain was sending. My brain commanded flee, get out of here, get away. But nothing was working. I heard my heart pounding in my ears, almost deafening. I felt suffocated. I tried to fight back. So helpless, I wanted to cry but no tears were coming. He had a smirk on his face. He kneed me in the stomach. I was on the ground. Blood poured from my finger from the cut he had made with his hunting knife, gushing onto the floor of the elevator. He sat on my back as I breathed heavily. He reached over and lifted my head to cover my mouth with his dirty sock that he had just removed from his shoe. My attacker turned me around. I looked at the eyes of the man who was going to kill me. The elevator opened, and I pushed myself away from him.

My fight or flight instincts in this experience was a combination of both. I fought as much as I could in the distress situation and managed to escape. I had a heavy heart, my stomach was filled with dread and my legs felt weak and numb. I didn't know if I would live to tell my story. The fight or flight process froze all my mental reasoning. I had nothing to draw upon. In those moments, I felt as if I was already dead.

"When a resolute young fellow steps up to the great bully, the world, and takes him boldly by the beard, he is often surprised to find it comes off in his hand, and that it was only tied on to scare away the timid adventurers."
— Ralph Waldo Emerson

It's so unlike running an ultramarathon, where I feel fear and butterflies, but running in the trails, hills, swamps - I have it under control. Time slows down and I am the master of my every step, barefoot. Although I have pain, I do not feel it. It's a different world. For me, I step into another reality. This is true empowerment. I can run contrary to the time when my life balanced on the edge of Martin's insanity and not one muscle would respond as I wished and needed.

Also, I don't tell many people this, but Amber's smile accompanies me on every run. She runs with me. I think back to the time after the attack when I couldn't walk and think of now when running is all my legs really know how to do.

Fear is not about being afraid. It's being afraid, but taking action anyhow. — Karl A Meninger

Just like Miobe carried a sack, I carry one too with my secret super-food to help me run the ultra-marathons. It's T.V.S. – the superfood of runners. Turmeric. Vinegar. Salt. Do you want to know what it really is?

Dr. Lycka: What are you talking about?

Harriet: I'll give you a hint. You eat it every time you have a hot dog."

Dr. Lycka: Mustard?

Harriet: On a run, it is my magic antidote to fight cramps and fear.

Dr. Lycka: Isn't that a contradiction? Yellow is often associated with cowards.

Harriet: Of course. yellow became associated with cowardice from the mid 13th century, when a group in the south of France was tried for heresy. This was known as the Albigensian Inquisition and was later incorporated into the Spanish Inquisition. The term "yellow belly" came out some time later as a derogatory term to refer to a coward.

Dr. Lycka: I'm impressed.

Harriet: Just trying to keep up with you Dr. Lycka. And with Dr. Google, it helps.

Dr. Lycka: Harriet, remember we talked about feeding the wolf? The wolf is often 'fear' and it takes over with this little voice inside your head that often keeps you stuck.

In general terms, it keeps us from getting what we want and prevents us from moving forward. Don't feed it with attention or analysis, like in the book *Feel the Fear and Do It Anyway*, a book by Susan Jeffers. You have heard the term 'paralyzed with fear'. It's very real. You felt it and lived it.

And it is present right now, seizing the world. As I write, a virus, COVID-19 is gripping the human race in wide-spread panic. It's spreading like wildfire across the globe. Mid-November, it struck Wuchan (Wuhan), China as the epicenter. To date, in China it has affected roughly about 85,000 and killed approximately 3,500. The Chinese have attempted to control its spread. It has incapacitated Italy, Spain and now the United States, especially New York, California and Massachusettes. It is striking Canada.

Doctors are using a primitive weapon – social distancing – a term much better referred to as physical distancing. People are sequestered to their homes which act like bunkers, and this is happening around the world. So far, 160 countries have been affected.

But this has been to little avail. Spread by international travel – cruise ships, airlines – it is fanned mainly by person to person and object to person touch. The virus is highly contagious.

Harriet: The buzzwords to protect are:

1. Wash your hands with soap and water to minimize your infection risk many times a day

2. Keep your hands away from your eyes, nose, and mouth.

3. Stay away from people who are coughing or sneezing.

4. Don't shake hands with people, whether they show symptoms or not.

5. Disinfect highly touched places.

6. Practice physical/social distancing to "flatten the curve." The last means the peak numbers of the epidemic are going to keep rising, the numbers increasing until people take it seriously. We can do our part and slow it down by listening to this advice.

Dr. Lycka: I'm also a big fan of wearing masks when in public.

This pandemic is scary, but the worst part of it is the fear that is gripping the nations. And controlling this fear will be important in managing this pandemic.

And, in the same vein, learning to manage fear and overcome it – even if that's sometimes just for 10 or 30 seconds so you can take an important action – is critical to *Living a Fantastic Life*. One of the baldest depictions of fear is a panic attack.

Harriet: Can we change the topic?

Dr. Lycka: Why?

Harriet: You are making me uncomfortable.

Dr. Lycka: I'm not understanding.

Harriet: Just because we're friends and I'm writing a book with you, doesn't mean I have to tell you all my secrets.

Dr. Lycka: The book is about secrets Harriet.

Harriet: Ughhh. You got me.

Dr. Lycka: Why am I making you uncomfortable?

Harriet: Please don't think badly about me. I am a sister, friend, volunteer, philanthropist, confidante, international model. I am caring, empathetic, thoughtful, amazing and all those great things you see.

But, there is something you cannot see. Some mornings, I get up and feel like I'm having a heart attack. I often feel like I'm drowning, I feel like I'm being pushed into my grave. I have this fear and cannot explain it. My heart races, I feel faint, some days I feel hot and distressed.

In those times, please don't judge me, don't fire me. Be patient with me. Don't tell me to get over it. Don't ask 'what's wrong with you', rather ask me what happened. That is my panic attack. This is not a form of mental illness. It is a symptom of an anxiety disorder. It is not physically dangerous. They are caused by the body's response to 'fight or flight' triggers. Most people will experience them at some point. It is critical that you speak to your general physician to get a customized plan.

Dr. Lycka: And they are surprisingly common. Most people experience a panic attack once or twice in their lives. The American Psychological Association reports that 1 out of every 75 people might experience a panic disorder.

Harriet: And I thought I was the only one.

Dr. Lycka: Well - you are special, but panic disorders are frighteningly common.

Harriet: I am not a fan of meds or herbal remedies. What I found works is CBT: Cognitive Behavioral Therapy. I'm not going to go into it much here, but it consists of;

1. recognizing it's occurring,

2. acknowledging that you're having one,

3. telling yourself that you will be okay,

4. slowing down your breathing,

5. focusing on your surroundings, and

6. releasing your tension by contracting and relaxing your muscles.

Dr Lycka: Wow. You said a lot. Take a deep cleansing breath.

"People living deeply have no fear of death." — *Anais Nin*

Now I will change the topic.

Did you know the Chinese symbol for 'crisis' has two parts.

Harriet: There you go Dr. Smarty Pants.

Dr. Lycka: Yup, I wear them proudly. Don't you like them?

Harriet: That gives me an idea for your next Christmas present – for the guy who has everything.

Dr. Lycka: Yeh, just like you – to take fear and make it into a designer line of clothes.

Harriet: Yup. I want to emulate Donna Karan.

Dr. Lycka: Good plan. We will launch that once we conquer fear. Let's get back on track – The traditional Chinese word for crisis is *pinyin*. It has two parts – one meaning danger and one meaning opportunity.

Harriet: I've learned you should concentrate on what you can control. Worrying about what you cannot control is a useless exercise.

Dr. Lycka: It sure is. It's like those late night infomercials, especially like Suzanne Somers with the thighmaster. Most useless piece of equipment and yet thousands bought into it. We are also making a choice when we buy into worry.

Harriet: Who said, all we have to fear is fear itself?

Dr. Lycka: Franklin Delano Roosevelt, during his first inauguration as the 32nd president of the United States, May 4, 1933.

Here's what he said: After taking the oath of office, Roosevelt proceeded to deliver his 1,883-word, 20 minute long inaugural address, best known for his famously pointed reference to 'fear itself' in one of its first lines:

"So, first of all, let me assert my firm belief that the only thing we have to fear is...fear itself — nameless, unreasoning, unjustified terror which paralyzes needed efforts to convert retreat into advance. In every dark hour of our national life a leadership of frankness and of vigor has met with that understanding and support of the people themselves which is essential to victory. And I am convinced that you will again give that support to leadership in these critical days."

The crisis of 1932 has a lot of parallels with the crisis of The Great

COVID-19 Pandemic of 2020.

In both, the stock markets had risen to unsustainable highs. Realizing this, Warren Buffet, chairman of Berkshire Hathaway, was sitting on 150 billion in cash as the crisis hit.

When the stock market fell in 1932, massive unemployment resulted. In the great pandemic of 2020, the same is holding true.

Roosevelt said, "*...the withered leaves of industrial enterprise lie on every side ...the savings of many years in thousands of families are gone.*

More important, a host of unemployed citizens face the grim problem of existence, and an equally great number toil with little return. Only a foolish optimist can deny the dark realities of the moment."

So, again, our greatest primary task is to put people to work.

Roosevelt said, "*There are many ways in which it can be helped, but it can never be helped merely by talking about it. We must act and act quickly.*"

Harriet: Yes. The words remind me that history repeats itself.

Dr. Lycka: And if we don't learn the lessons of history, we will always be its victim.

Harriet: Well said.

Dr. Lycka: I won't let you get away with the last word this time. It's mine.

Harriet: No you won't. We both will.

This book was completed during the Great Pandemic of 2020.

The seed was started years earlier, but - just as a seed takes time to grow - so did this book. It was written alone, together in coffee shops – like Starbucks, The Carrot Cafe and The Portugese Bakery all in Edmonton, Alberta. We wrote it at Jack Canfield's house in San Bernardino, California. And members of the press contributed to it at Steve Harrison's National Publicity Summit in New York City. Finally, when the COVID-19 virus fire blazed across North America, the book was virtually completed.

But back in December, 2019 a disaster happened. Dr. Lycka inadvertently left his computer and briefcase behind his car and drove over them both. The computer was destroyed. However, Dr. Lycka had sent many versions to Harriet and to the icloud, which ended up saving the day.

Fear is a bit like dancing – you are enveloped by the music, so you dance to it. But to conquer fear, you must surrender to it. — Dr. Allen Lycka

CONCLUSION

The theme of this book is not what happens to you. It's what you do with what happens. Just as Harriet and I both experienced adversity, we know we are not alone. And neither are you. We are here to journey with you offering our golden pearls.

Please feel free to write to us with your own adversity stories. Stay tuned for future editions in which your stories may appear as an integral part to shine a light for others who are waiting to hear how you have overcome.

Courage is what it takes to stand up and speak; courage is also what it takes to sit down and listen.
— Winston Churchill

We plan to roll out another book every four to six months. You can find out more by going to www.drallenlycka.com.

QUOTES USED IN THIS BOOK

No book written in 2020 can claim to have *The Secrets of Living A Fantastic Life* without being influenced by the thoughts and words of many others. These are some of the words and thoughts. Some of these were so good, they made it to the body of this book. Others, for various reasons, made it to the cutting room floor. Still others will find their place in further versions of this book.

Enjoy!

1) "Love – I believe that dreaming is stronger than reality. Desire is more potent than apathy. Hopes are more powerful than despair. Joy always triumphs over sorrow. Laughter is the ultimate cure for mankind's foibles. And I believe that love is stronger than hate and is the greatest gift of all. How do I know? I have been fortunate to experience them all." - Dr. Allen Lycka

2) "You always gain by giving love." - Reese Witherspoon

3) "Believe in love. Believe in magic. Hell, believe in Santa Claus. Believe in others. Believe in yourself. Believe in your dreams. If you don't, who will?" - Jon Bon Jovi

4) "My favourite thing in life is writing about life, specifically the

parts of life concerning love. Because, as far as I'm concerned, love is absolutely everything." - Taylor Swift

5) "If you love until it hurts, there can be no more hurt, only more love." - Mother Teresa

6) "Love is a force more formidable than any other. It is invisible – it cannot be seen or measured, yet it is powerful enough to transform you in a moment and offer you more joy than any material possession could." - Barbara De Angelis

7) "And in the end, the love you take, is equal to the love you make." - Paul McCartney

8) "Live an inspired life. Be 'the inspiration' for someone else. Accept the inspiration given to you." - Harriet Tinka

9) "In life you need either inspiration or desperation." - Tony Robbins

10) People think, "If I could only get motivated, then I'll act. Nope. In actuality, it's the opposite." - Brendon Burchard

11) "Success is liking yourself, liking what you do and liking how you do it." - Mary Tyler Moore

12) "My great hope is to laugh as much as I cry; to get my work done and try to love somebody and have the courage to accept the love in return." - Maya Angelou

13) "There is no passion to be found playing small – in settling for a life that is less than the one you are capable of living." - Nelson Mandela

14) "There is winning and there is misery." - Bill Parcells

15) "Winning is the most important thing in my life, after breathing. Breathing first, winning next." - George Steinbrenner

16) "Nothing is black-and-white, except for winning and losing, and maybe that's why people gravitate to that so much." - Steve Nash

17) "Winning is not a sometime thing; it's an all-time thing. You

don't win once in a while, you don't do things right once in a while, you do them right all the time. Winning is habit. Unfortunately, so is losing." - Vince Lombardi

18) "Vulnerability is the birthplace of love, belonging, joy, courage, empathy, and creativity. It is the source of hope, empathy, accountability, and authenticity." - Brené Brown, Daring Greatly: How the Courage to Be Vulnerable Transforms the Way We Live, Love, Parent, and Lead

19) "Vulnerability is basically uncertainty, risk, and emotional exposure." - Brene Brown

20) "Victory is sweetest when you've known defeat." - Malcolm Forbes

21) "Honesty and transparency make you vulnerable. Be honest and transparent anyway." - Mother Teresa

22) "I understand now that the vulnerability I've always felt is the greatest strength a person can have. You can't experience life without feeling life." - Elisabeth Shue

23) "Vulnerability is the birthplace of love, belonging, joy, courage, and creativity. It is the source of hope, empathy, accountability, and authenticity. If we want greater clarity in our purpose or deeper or more meaningful spiritual lives, vulnerability is the path." - Brené Brown

24) "Honesty and transparency make you vulnerable. Be honest and transparent anyway." - Mother Teresa

25) "I understand now that the vulnerability I've always felt is the greatest strength a person can have. You can't experience life without feeling life. What I've learned is that being vulnerable to somebody you love is not a weakness, it's a strength." - Elisabeth Shue

26) "I believe we're all put on this planet for a purpose. When you connect with that love and that compassion, that's when everything unfolds." - Ellen DeGeneres

27) "Everybody has a purpose." - Dolly Parton

28) "The purpose of life is not to be happy. It is to be useful, to be honourable, to be compassionate, to have it make some difference that you have lived and lived well." - Ralph Waldo Emerson

29) "What is success? I think it is a mixture of having a flair for the thing that you are doing; knowing that it is not enough, that you have got to have hard work and a certain sense of purpose." - Margaret Thatcher

30) "Definiteness of purpose is the starting point of all achievement." - W. Clement Stone

31) "The wise treat self-respect as non-negotiable, and will not trade it for health or wealth or anything else." - Thomas Szasz

32) "Non-negotiables are essential pearls of success. They are a key to living. They define what you will never compromise on." - Dr. Allen Lycka

33) "Non-negotiables are a line in the sand." - Harriet Tinka

34) "Do not negotiate your dignity or freedoms: both are non-negotiable." - Mohammed Sekouty

35) "Trust and truth are not negotiable." - Dr. Allen Lycka

36) "Beauty begins when you learn to love yourself." - Harriet Tinka

37) "Non-negotiables give the driving force for life." - Dr. Allen Lycka

38) "When we know what's essential in our lives, everything else is negotiable. What are some things you don't do?" - Shauna Niequist

39) "Life is based on 13 Golden Pearls." - Harriet Tinka

40) "As we know, forgiveness of oneself is the hardest of all." - Joan Baez

41) "There would be no need for love if perfection were possible. Love arises from our imperfection." - Eugene Kennedy

42) "Darkness cannot drive out darkness; only light can do that. Hate cannot drive out hate; only love can do that." - Martin Luther King

43) "Forgiveness is not always easy. At times, it feels more painful than the wound we suffered, to forgive the one that inflicted it. And yet, there is no peace without forgiveness." - Marianne Williamson

44) "We make a living by what we get, but we make a life by what we give." - Winston Churchill

45) "We're all in this together. Each and every one of us can make a difference by giving back." - Beyoncé, Professional singer, musician and founder of BeyGoo

46) "If you're in the luckiest one percent of humanity, you owe it to the rest of humanity to think about the other 99 percent." - Warren Buffet, Investor, businessman and member of The Giving Pledge

47) "Is the rich world aware of how four billion of the six billion live? If we were aware, we would want to help out, we'd want to get involved." – Bill Gates, business magnate, computer programmer and co-founder of the Bill and Melinda Gates Foundation

48) "Living is Giving. Give until it hurts then give some more." - Dr. Allen Lycka

49) "Wherever you go, go with all your heart." You can make a difference. The world of selfless giving is full of wonderfulness. I wish want you to experience the joy of seeing smiles on others faces." - Confucius

50) "He who gives love, receives love." - Omar Torrijos Herrera

51) "I try to keep it real. I don't have time to worry about what I'm projecting to the world. I'm just busy being myself." - Demi Lovato

52) "I'm happy being myself, which I've never been before. I always hid in other people, or tried to find myself through the

characters, or live out their lives, but I didn't have those things in mine." - Angelina Jolie

53) "I had everything I'd hoped for, but I wasn't being myself. So, I decided to be honest about who I was. It was strange: The people who loved me for being funny suddenly didn't like me for being... me." - Ellen DeGeneres

54) "I am not who you think I am; I am not who I think I am; I am who I think you think I am." - Thomas Cooley

55) "Forgiveness is not always easy. At times, it feels more painful than the wound we suffered, to forgive the one that inflicted it." - Marianne Williamson

56) "There would be no need for love if perfection were possible. Love arises from our imperfection." - Eugene Kennedy

57) "Darkness cannot drive out darkness; only light can do that. Hate cannot drive out hate; only love can do that."- Martin Luther King

58) "Forgiveness is giving up the hope that the past could have been any different, it's accepting the past for what it was, and using this moment and this time to help yourself move forward." - Oprah Winfrey

59) "Mistakes are always forgivable, if one has the courage to admit them." - Bruce Lee

60) "You play the hand you're dealt. I think the game's worthwhile." - Christopher Reeve

61) "Be cheerful, positive, and determined - you will go far!" - Earl Nightingale

62) "Being a sex symbol has to do with an attitude, not looks. Most men think It's looks, most women know otherwise." - Kathleen Turner

63) "Attitude is absolutely everything in life! The only thing more contagious than a good attitude is a bad one." - David Goggins

64) "My attitude is that: if you push me towards something that you think is a weakness, then I will turn that perceived weakness into a strength." - Michael Jordan

65) "Funny is an attitude." - Flip Wilson

66) "Being thankful for this breath in and out of my lungs, knowing that this will one day cease, is what keeps my heart beating for the next smile, the next sunrise, and the sound of the next little girl's giggle." - Dr. Allen Lycka

67) "Living in a state of gratitude is the gateway to grace." - Arianna Huffington.

68) "I cried because I had no shoes until I met a man who had no feet." - Author unknown

69) "I practice the Oprah Winfrey ritual: I check in with gratitude and grace when I wake up. I can be in a state of overwhelm." - Kerry Washington

70) "I try to start every day and end every day by taking a moment to be grateful." - Olivia Wilde

71) "When I started counting my blessings, my whole life turned around." - Willie Nelson

72) "Gratitude is the closest thing to beauty manifested in an emotion." - Mindy Kaling

73) "I'm tenacious. I think - I know - and I do also have a quality where if you tell me I can't do something, if I know I can't do it, I'm the first to raise my hand and say, 'I can't do that.' But there is a big Bronx New York Jew in me that says, 'Really? You think 'Yes I can...Yes I can do it. I Can Do It !!!!'" - Ellen Barkin

74) "I play to win, whether during practice or a real game. And I will not let anything get in the way of me and my competitive enthusiasm to win." - Michael Jordan

75) "Enthusiasm is a volcano on whose top never grows the grass of hesitation." - Kahlil Gibran

76) "The more you trust your intuition, the more empowered you become, and the happier you become." - Gisele Bundchen

77) "I don't like to gamble but if there's one thing I'm willing to bet on, it's myself." - Beyonce

78) "You will not determine my story, I will." - Amy Schumer

79) "Whether you think you can, or you think you can't –you're right." - Henry Ford

80) "Let food be thy medicine and medicine be thy food." - Hippocrates

81) "You are what you eat," - quoting his mother, David Friedman Food Sanity: How to Eat in a World of Fads and Fiction, 2018

82) "Food is medicine – what we eat has a profound effect on our health." - Harvey Diamond Fit For Life

83) "And when all feels hopeless, remember that you are in charge of what goes into your body, you don't answer to anyone, and you are allowed to eat anything you want. Often just knowing we can eat whatever we want is enough to keep us from eating whatever we want. We're so rebellious." - Rory Freedman, Skinny Bitch: A No-Nonsense, Tough-Love Guide for Savvy Girls Who Want to Stop Eating Crap and Start Looking Fabulous!

84) "For a slim, sexy body, it's important to eat protein every day - preferably at every meal. Be sure to ask about the origins of your meat, poultry and seafood." - Suzanne Somers

85) "Abundance is the quality of life you live and quality of life you give to others." - J.K. Rowling

86) "Today expect something good to happen to you no matter what occurred yesterday. Realize the past no longer holds you captive. It can only continue to hurt you if you hold on to it. Let the past go. A simply abundant world awaits." - Sarah Ban Breathnach, Simple Abundance: A Daybook of Comfort and Joy

87) "A generous heart filled with gratitude is a magnet for abundance." - Debasish Mridha

88) "In a growth mindset, people believe that their most basic abilities can be developed through dedication and hard work – brains and talent are just the starting point. This view creates a love of learning and a resilience that is essential for great accomplishment." - Carol Dweck, Mindset: The New Psychology of Success

89) "Expect abundance to receive abundance." - Debasish Mridha

90) "Every man lives in two realms: the internal and the external. The internal is that realm of spiritual ends expressed in art, literature, morals, and religion. The external is that complex of devices, techniques, mechanisms, and instrumentalities by means of which we live." - Martin Luther King, Jr.

91) "Just as a candle cannot burn without fire, we cannot live without a spiritual life." - Buddha

92) "Spirituality is your inner face: it is your discovery of your inner nature." - Osho

93) "Being spiritual has nothing to do with what you believe and everything to do with your state of consciousness." - Eckhart Tolle

94) "I believe that having a spiritual life is so important in everybody's life." - Lou Holtz

95) "What is tenacity? The act of being persistent. Now, what is persistence? Persistence is stick-to-it-tiveness." - Dr. Allen Lycka

96) "If you are determined enough and willing to pay the price, you can get it done." - Mike Ditka

97) "What is tenacity? The act of being persistent. Now, what is persistence? Persistence is tenacity." - Dr. Allen Lycka

98) "People of mediocre ability sometimes achieve outstanding success because they don't know when to quit. Most men succeed because they are determined to." - George Allan

99) "People of mediocre ability sometimes achieve outstanding success because they don't know when to quit. Most men suc-

ceed because they are determined to." - George Allan

100) "Many of life's failures are people who did not realize how close they were to success when they gave up." - Thomas A. Edison

101) "You are the only problem you have ever had and you are the only solution you will ever have." - Bob Proctor

102) "An onion can make people cry but there's never been a vegetable that can make people laugh." - Will Rogers

103) "You can't deny laughter; when it comes, it plops down in your favorite chair and stays as long as it wants." - Stephen King

104) "It is not success that brings enthusiasm. It is the enthusiasm that brings success." - Ralph Waldo Emerson

105) "Enthusiasm glows, radiates, permeates and immediately captures everyone's interest." - Paul Meyer

106) "My mom always used to say, 'You can't say I love you before you can say I.' And I think that sort of makes sense." - Mindy Kailing

107) "There's nothing more intimate in life than simply being understood. And understanding someone else." - Brad Meltzer

108) "Fear is the great enemy of intimacy. Fear makes us run away from each other or cling to each other but does not create true intimacy." - Henri Nouwen

109) "Passion is the quickest to develop, and the quickest to fade. Intimacy develops more slowly, and commitment more gradually still." - Robert Sternberg

110) "Love is a decision, not just an emotion. It is selfless, and a commitment." - Lydia McLaughlin

111) "Courage is being scared to death, and saddling up anyway." - John Wayne

112) "Without courage, we cannot practice any other virtue with consistency. We can't be kind, true, merciful, generous, or

honest." - Dr. Maya Angelou

113) "It's not what happens to you, it's what you do with what happens." - Chris Waddell

114) "And most important, have the courage to follow your heart and intuition. They somehow already know what you truly want to become. Everything else is secondary." - Steve Jobs

115) "It takes courage...to endure the sharp pains of self-discovery rather than choose to take the dull pain of unconsciousness that would last the rest of our lives." - Marianne Williamson, "Return to Love: Reflections on the Principles of 'A Course in Miracles'"

116) "Being terrified but going ahead and doing what must be done – that's courage. The one who feels no fear is a fool, and the one who lets fear rule him is a coward." - Piers Anthony

117) "Sometimes standing against evil is more important than defeating it. The greatest heroes stand because it is right to do so, not because they believe they will walk away with their lives. Such selfless courage is a victory in itself." - N.D. Wilson, Dandelion Fire

118) An onion can make people cry but there's never been a vegetable that can make people laugh. - Will Rogers

119) "[Humanity] has unquestionably one weapon—laughter. Power, money, persuasion, supplication, persecution – these can lift at a colossal humbug – push it a little – weaken it a little, century by century, but only laughter can blow it to rags and atoms at a blast. Against the assault of laughter nothing can stand." - Mark Twain

120) "I always knew looking back on my tears would bring me laughter, but I never knew looking back on my laughter would make me cry." - Cat Stevens

121) "Remember laughing? Laughter enhances the blood flow to the body's extremities and improves cardiovascular function. Laughter releases endorphins and other natural mood elevating and pain-killing chemicals improves the transfer of oxygen and

nutrients to internal organs. Laughter boosts the immune system and helps the body fight off disease, cancer cells as well as viral, bacterial and other infections. Being happy is the best cure of all diseases!" - Patch Adams

122) "Dare to say no. Have the courage to face the truth. Please do the right thing because it is right. These are the magic keys to living your life with integrity." - W. Clement Stone

123) "With integrity, you have nothing to fear, since you have nothing to hide. With integrity, you will do the right thing so that you will have no guilt." - Zig Ziglar

124) "As I have said, the first thing is, to be honest with yourself. You can never have an impact on society if you have not changed yourself. Great peacemakers are all people of integrity, of honesty, but humility." - Nelson Mandela

125) "Success Is Going from Failure to Failure Without Losing Your Enthusiasm." - Sir Winston Churchill

126) "It's failure that gives you the proper perspective on success." - Ellen DeGeneres

127) "Failure is so important. We speak about success all the time. It is the ability to resist failure or use failure that often leads to greater success. I've met people who don't want to try for fear of failing." - J.K. Rowling

128) "When we give ourselves permission to fail, we, at the same time, give ourselves permission to excel." - Eloise Ristad

129) "Success is failing nine times and getting up ten." - Jon Bon Jovi

130) "Enthusiasm glows, radiates, permeates and immediately captures everyone's interest." - Paul J. Meyer

131) "Enthusiasm is a volcano on whose top never grows the grass of hesitation." - Kahlil Gibran

132) "Confidence and empowerment are cousins in my opinion. Empowerment comes from within and typically it's stemmed

and fostered by self-assurance. To feel empowered is to feel free and that's when people do their best work. You can't fake confidence or empowerment." - Amy Jo Martin

133) "The process of spotting fear and refusing to obey it is the source of all true empowerment." - Martha Beck

134) "In the end, people will judge you anyway, so don't live your life impressing others – live your life impressing yourself." - Eunice Infante

135) "People living deeply have no fear of death." - Anais Nin

136) "When a resolute young fellow steps up to the great bully, the world, and takes him boldly by the beard, he is often surprised to find it comes off in his hand, and that it was only tied on to scare away the timid adventurers." - Ralph Waldo Emerson

137) "Fear is the main source of superstition, and one of the main sources of cruelty. To conquer fear is the beginning of wisdom." - Bertrand Russell

138) "Fears are educated into us, and can, if we wish, be educated out." - Karl A. Menninger

139) "Fear is not about being afraid. It's being afraid, but taking action anyhow." - Dr. Allen Lycka

140) "Too many people are thinking of security instead of opportunity. They seem to be more afraid of life than death." - James F. Byrnes

141) "Courage is what it takes to stand up and speak; courage is also what it takes to sit down and listen." - Winston Churchill

142) "Fear is a bit like dancing – you are enveloped by the music so you dance to it. But to conquer fear, you must surrender to it." - Dr. Allen Lycka

143) "I must not fear. Fear is the mind-killer. Fear is the little-death that brings total obliteration. I will face my fear. I will permit it to pass over me and through me. And when it has gone past I will turn the inner eye to see its path. Where the fear has

gone there will be nothing. Only I will remain." - Frank Herbert, Dune

144) "There are two basic motivating forces: fear and love. When we are afraid, we pull back from life. When we are in love, we open to all that life has to offer with passion, excitement, and acceptance. We need to learn to love ourselves first, in all our glory and our imperfections. If we cannot love ourselves, we cannot fully open to our ability to love others or our potential to create. Evolution and all hopes for a better world rest in the fearlessness and open-hearted vision of people who embrace life." - John Lennon

THANK YOU

A book of this complexity cannot be made without the help of dozens, even hundreds of individuals. My deepest gratitude to all those listed below who made this book a success. Thank you.
- *Dr. Allen Lycka*

Aaliyah Davis
A Mark Joffe
Aaron Bjorndal
Aaron McCalla
Ali Salman
Alice Tinka
Alison Clarke
Allan Behm
Amaya Ortigosa
Bonnie Caton
Brenda Dintiman
Brent Collingwood
Bruce Kirkland
Calvin Lim
Career Alternatives
Cecile R Lavoie
Charles Crutchfield
Cheryl Davis
Chris Stasniak
Christine Huget

Christine Molnar
Christopher Gowers
Clifford Neufeld
Cloudowl Inc.
Cynthia Dusseault
Darryl Humphrey
Dary Frunchak
Daryl Hoffman
David Adam
David Holdsworth
David Kinnaird
David Martz
Dean Wood
Denis R Vincent
Donald Bladen
Donald McGarvey
Donna Davis
Doug Rutherford
Dr. Peter Ursel
Duff Robison

Earl Campbell
Elaine Zimmer
Eva Strecheniuk
Evelyne Tinka
Evert Tuyp
Fred Tinka
Gabriela Radu
Genevieve Mayberry
George Hruza
George Sexsmith
Gordon Searles
Hans Von Bloedau
Harry Buddl
Ihsan Sassi
James Baumgaertner
Jason Anderson
Jean Bitakinsanga
Jeff McCann
Jennifer Cantrell
Jess Vivier
Jimmy Lefebvre
Jimmy Tinka
J'lyn Nye
Joe Lycka
Joel Schlessinger
Nancy Schlessinger
John Bailey
John Middleton
John Williams
Judy Harcourt Brown
Justin & Jacquie Duval
Karen Bennett
Kelly Osaka
Leslie Cleary
Linda Bartlett
Lindsay Robinson
Lola Ibraimova
Lora Lee Peaslee
Lucie Bernier-Lycka
Luis Nader

Lyle Best
Marc Guberti
Mark Bayrock
Martin Mugambi
MegaBucks Marketing, Inc.
Michael Vivier
Michelle Jeannotte
Miles Gibson
Mitchell Hill
Neal Bailey
Neil Cockburn
Nelson Scott
Nicholas Fu
Nicholas Tinka
Noga Liron
Noreen Kompanik
Norman Johnson
Nur Lakhani
Pamela Jenkins
Paul Dusseault
Perry Marshall Marketing
Systems Inc.
Peter Lynch
Philip Tinka
Ravi Padarath
Rhiannah Davis
Robert McNaught
Roderick Keats
Roman Bayrock
Ron Low
Rose Tinka
RTP Advertising Agency, Inc
Rusti L Lehay, Collaborative
Editor
Ryan Deiss
Ryan Sellers
Sandra McDonald
Selina Gray
Selvakumar Munuswamy
Sharon Hill

Sheldon Hendricks
Stephanie MacDonald
Stephen Lau
Steve Davis
Susan Ritter
Suzanne Depledge
Svetlana Pavlenko
Tamara Klein
Tamaralyn McCalla
Tamisan Bencz-Knight
Tara Candido
Thaddeus Winston
Thomas Greidanus
Thomas Hill
Tristan Schultenkamper
Una Mulvany
Vera Bozunovic
Wayne Kauffman
William Betteridge
William Ohe
Your Holistic Earth
Zaki Taher
Zulfikar Lila

We'd also like to thank Lauren Magliaro for contributing her story "My Uncle" to our book, *The Secrets to Living a Fantastic Life...*

Lauren lives in Rockaway NJ with her husband, son and Goldendoodle. She loves Springsteen the NY Yankees, reading and Disney World. Her background is in Marketing but writing is her dream career. Her ultimate goal is to write a "tween" book.

The Last Words

Harriet and I would like to thank you for reading our book and sharing our journey.

We've really enjoyed sharing. As you probably realize, we have not been able to cover everything.

This book began as *The Secrets of Living a Fantastic Life ... Discovery of the 20 Golden Pearls*. We cut it down to 13 because it was just too overwhelming. So, in the near future, we will have a second book with more delightful golden pearls of wisdom: more stories, more quotes and more joy to enhance your life.

But this book is not just about our journey. It really is about your journey and we want to help you on it. So we have two amazing bonuses for you:

1. Text me "Golden Pearls" to 1-819-717-2515 and I will send you a golden pearl a week to enhance your life
2. Send in the subject line "Golden Pearls" to DrAllenLycka@gmail.com and we will schedule you a free 15 minute consultation to help you discover how *The Secrets of Living a Fantastic Life* can enhance your life, each and every day.
3. To find out how your story might appear as a pearl in future books, please schedule a free call as noted above.

Thank you – have a "FANTASTIC DAY"!

Dr. Allen Lycka and Harriet Tinka